CONQUERING CHAOS! 8 KEYS TO MASTER EXECUTIVE FUNCTION AND LIFE SKILLS FOR TEENS WITH ADHD

MANAGE THE CHAOS THROUGH UNDERSTANDING YOUR MIND AND USING PRACTICAL STRATEGIES TO IMPROVE YOUR MENTAL AND PHYSICAL WELLBEING.

SELENEA KNIGHT

CONTENTS

INTRODUCTION

Do you ever get the feeling that you're not normal or that there's something wrong with you? You've always done things differently than your friends or classmates, and you can't seem to get your ducks in a row. Well, that's because if you have ADHD or an executive function deficit (EFD), you are classified as neurodivergent, meaning your brain works and processes information differently than is considered typical.

Being neurodivergent is not a bad thing, though it can be hard to keep up with others your age in a world where everything is geared towards neurotypicals. You are expected to sit quietly and soak up all this information every day for hours on end even though, more often than not, people with ADHD are physically incapable of doing so.

The truth is that everyone's brain is slightly different, which is why research on neurodivergence is so complex and debated. Because if everyone's mind processes information differently, how do you determine what is typical and what isn't?

However, I think everyone will agree with me that always living on either end of the extreme is not typical or helpful. You're either talking too much or not at all, studying for eight hours straight without eating, drinking water, or taking a break, or not studying at all. You might randomly find the energy and motivation to deep clean your entire room, rearrange the furniture, and reorganize all the drawers and your entire cupboard, but then you spend days feeling exhausted with not enough energy to even make your bed or brush your teeth.

What's even worse is you tend to hyperfocus on the wrong things. You have a four-page essay to write, but you feel like you can't start on that before you've washed your sneakers and put away the clean laundry. This can be extremely frustrating, especially since you never have the energy or motivation when you actually need it.

On top of all that, you might have problems starting on a task because of an executive function deficit (or EFD). That is when no matter how much you urge yourself to start doing something, you just can't. Your parents may just classify this as being lazy, which can negatively affect your self-esteem since you have every intention of doing it, but you just can't get started for some inexplicable reason.

The difference between being lazy and executive dysfunction is intention. Laziness is when you know exactly what to do, you have the energy and capacity to do it with little effort, yet you choose to procrastinate because you don't feel like doing it at the moment. Executive dysfunction is when you want to do it, but you just end up staring into space, feeling like you're paralyzed in your own body. A lot of factors can contribute to this: you might not know how or where to start, you don't have the motivation or energy to do it, you're overwhelmed, or you can't bring yourself to focus on the task for long enough to get anything done.

Unfortunately, there is no cure for ADHD or executive dysfunction. But there are treatments and many ways to combat the sometimes crippling symptoms of these disorders and make life just a little easier to cope with.

That's exactly what will be explored in this book. Besides encouraging you to accept your struggles and mental differences, you will learn many possible strategies on how you can retrain your brain and set yourself up for success despite your neurological disorder.

A thorough breakdown of what exactly ADHD and executive dysfunction are will help you understand your own brain better as well as make you aware of how these disorders can create thought patterns and habits that impact everyday situations adversely.

You will learn how to take back control over your emotions and practice mindfulness to minimize the chaos that's usually going on in your head. Mind clutter can worsen symptoms of ADHD and executive dysfunction by increasing anxiety, disrupting sleep, and interfering with memory and attention span. This is why it's important to know how to avoid it or manage it when it does happen.

Creating habits that help you stay regulated and organized can be great as long as you're not too hard on yourself for not sticking with a certain program or schedule. Organizing your life is more about creating a guideline while still keeping in mind that life doesn't ask for permission to happen. It doesn't come naturally to everyone, and that's okay. You can always adapt a regime or strategy to suit your preferences and lifestyle in a way that is practical and realistic.

Probably the most important thing to address is how taking care of yourself can improve and help manage your symptoms. Self-care is non-negotiable. I think people always assume that everyone knows how to take care of themselves, but that's not the case. This book will outline everything you need to know about taking care of your physical and mental well-being.

Your productivity depends on your ability to budget and organize your time, solve problems, and be mentally flexible, which is why there is a whole chapter dedicated to these factors and how you can develop these respective skills.

Many teenagers with ADHD often struggle with balancing school and home life on top of having a thriving social life. Throughout this book, you will learn how to avoid getting overwhelmed with everything going on at school while still having enjoyable hobbies and socializing with friends.

But most important of all, you will learn ways to bypass executive functioning deficits and essentially rewire your brain to be better able to initiate tasks by setting realistic goals, breaking them down, and achieving them.

I have worked in plenty of fields relating to healthcare. But my passion has always been working with children and teens with emotional and behavioral trouble, as well as mental health disorders.

Because my parents took in so many young foster kids into our home with me and my brother, I have learned to be nurturing, compassionate, and understanding towards them and their struggles. My priority is to create an environment where children and teenagers feel comfortable and safe to express their thoughts and feelings freely.

Everyone deserves that, but not everyone is able to provide it. As our understanding and research of mental disorders continue to grow, many people are still set in their misconceptions of it. They might not feel the need to educate themselves since their lives are not being affected by it directly.

I know it's an unfair burden that we have to inform others, in addition to coping with something as complex as ADHD or executive function deficit. However, denying the facts won't improve our position, health, or well-being. There are many campaigns whose initiatives are geared towards bringing awareness to the battles that neurodivergent people face every day of their lives.

Due to challenges with my own health, I am no longer able to continue my career in a professional capacity in the healthcare system. However, I am still determined to help children and teens live a life where they don't feel rejected or alone just because they think differently. Through utilizing my education and experience, I remain optimistic that I am still able to help others to some degree.

My goal with the book is to provide you with the knowledge and tools that might bring some relief when facing the obstacles in life due to neurodiversity on top of all the changes in your body as you grow into adulthood so that you can thrive even if you have limited support.

Just because other people can't grasp how difficult it is or don't support you, doesn't mean you don't deserve it. Being your own advocate is the most important life skill that anyone can have. Even when you're being fed negativity and judgment from all angles, you can still ground yourself and believe your truth.

1

COME TO TERMS WITH YOUR IDENTITY

Getting a diagnosis can be helpful, but it's not always necessary. This subject is heavily debated, but I want to share my thoughts on it. Everything related to psychology is typically a spectrum. You might have ADHD traits but not meet the criteria to be formally diagnosed, however, that doesn't diminish your reality.

I'm not suggesting you go on the internet and believe the first quiz on ADHD that gives you a positive result. Self-diagnosing is way more complicated and involves a ridiculous amount of research and self-awareness.

A diagnosis is also important to be able to receive treatment if needed. Usually, mild forms of ADHD are treated with therapy and support, while more severe forms of ADHD require medications in addition to this.

That being said, even if you don't have a diagnosis and you believe that you might be having symptoms of ADHD or EFD, coming to terms with it is the first step towards self-acceptance and improvement.

You Are the Manager of Your Brain

Life is always happening, and with social media giving you access to all the information all of the time, it can be hard to control what information is prioritized in your mind. The good news is you are in charge of your brain, or at least you can be.

Learning to concentrate and determining what to focus on and when can be extremely valuable. No one on earth can solve every single problem in the world at once. It's your job as the manager of your brain to try your best to understand how your mind works, overcome challenges, and improve to be the best version of yourself.

How ADHD Affects the Brain

Knowing how ADHD and EFD affect you is important. These neurological disorders can affect you in ways you didn't even know were related. When you do some research, you find common symptoms, such as the inability to focus or concentrate, hyperactivity, impulsivity, being easily distracted, forgetfulness, inability to follow instructions, always fidgeting, interrupting others often, and jumping from task to task.

But ADHD can also cause you to be overcritical of yourself, leading to a negative self-image. It can induce bouts of anxiety or insomnia that can affect your physical well-being and lead to constant physical and mental fatigue, which then further worsens the symptoms associated with ADHD. You might be emotionally sensitive and have frequent breakdowns that go on for days. Because of your ADHD traits, you might come across as insensitive, uncaring, and irresponsible to others, and this might cause friction in your close relationships.

Your brain is made up of various compartments and networks, and they all communicate with each other through chemical messages (neurotransmitters such as endorphins and hormones). When you have ADHD or EFD, the neurological pathways in your brain don't form at the same rate that neurotypical brains do. Also, your brain might not be producing enough of these neurotransmitters (specifically dopamine), meaning your brain isn't able to effectively process or react to information and stimuli.

Neurotransmitters such as dopamine, serotonin, and noradrenaline are responsible for stabilizing mood and internal reward responses. With ADHD or EFD, your brain is unable to release the feel-good endorphins that motivate you to continue working hard or start on a new task. Unfortunately, this also means you probably have a tough time regulating your own emotions.

So not only does your brain take longer to develop, but you may also have trouble making decisions, learning or starting new tasks, prioritizing, and organizing your thoughts.

How to Take Back Control

The ADHD brain loves repeating thought patterns. While it's possible to rewire your mind and take control of your thoughts, these thoughts are relentless and much harder to change. Plus, it can sometimes feel like you have multiple streams of consciousness playing over each other in a constant loop.

Some people describe it as having a beehive in their heads, just constant buzzing all the time. Other people describe it as having multiple voices in their heads, but all of the voices are their own. For example, one voice is planning the next day, one is shaming you for not cleaning your room, one is singing a single verse of a song over and over again, and one is narrating everything that happened to you this morning. It's no wonder you're unable to focus.

It's even harder if you're sensitive to audible stimuli and get overwhelmed easily. You have to go through life with all this chaos in your mind and take on the world, which in and of itself can be a lot to deal with.

What usually tends to happen is something triggers you, leading to your mind spiraling with scenarios, assumptions, and distorted perspectives that leave you feeling paralyzed and dysregulated. It happens to everyone, but people with ADHD and EFD are more susceptible to these triggers and less able to re-regulate themselves when they do occur.

And while you can't stop triggers or negative thoughts from entering your mind, you can work on breaking the cycle so that you don't feel like your whole world is caving in with every minor inconvenience that happens to you.

Distracting yourself with school, friends, and entertainment can help give you a temporary break from the constant stream of thoughts frying your brain, though it's not very helpful in the long run as a sole solution.

However, there are a few things you can try that might help calm your anxious, speeding thoughts.

Figure Out Your Triggers

Knowing what initially causes your brain to freak out can help you prepare for the aftermath. If you recognize that pressure or stress, such as exams, worsen your ADHD, you can mentally prepare yourself for it. Alternatively, many things can trigger these spiraling thought patterns; sleep deprivation, overstimulation, caffeine, and even LCD screens like phones and computers can have an impact.

Simply observe your symptoms and try to pinpoint what thought or event triggered you and write it down (because you will forget). Negative thoughts are inevitable, so don't sit around anxiously waiting for them to happen. The trigger itself isn't the main issue—it's how you respond to it. By being aware of your triggers, you can work on preventing your emotional response.

Name Your Emotional Responses

Admitting to yourself, whether out loud or in your mind, what you are feeling or experiencing can stop the cycle of endless thoughts by separating your subconscious from your conscious mind.

When you feel like your thoughts are headed toward a dark place, try to put your feelings into words. This can be as simple as telling yourself, "I am overwhelmed by the noise of the crowd of people," "I am stressed because I haven't started on that project yet and it's due tomorrow," or "I am frustrated because I can't get started on this task."

It could also extend to physical responses that can occur as a result of emotional responses. For example, "I feel light-headed because I am overstimulated," "My heart is beating fast because I am anxious," or "I feel depressed because today was a bad day."

Naming your emotional state can also help you get in touch with your emotions and recognize patterns on a deeper level.

Reality Check

You've spent hours creating and obsessing over the worst possible scenarios and outcomes imaginable. But what are the chances of them actually happening in real life? The mind believes what you continuously feed it. Therefore, every time you tell yourself something you believe it a bit more. This is also true when other people keep telling you something is objectively false such as "you're just lazy." It's called gaslighting, and eventually, you will start to believe it to be true.

This strategy can be used in a positive and negative aspect. If you tell yourself that you're going to pass the test even though you didn't study, you'll believe you're going to pass, but in reality, there's a big chance you might fail, and vice versa. Try to remind yourself of the facts instead of just assuming the worst.

In most cases, relying on your assumptions is not reliable, and it takes some serious brain power to put yourself in a position where you're not biased or catastrophizing the situation. Sometimes it's just easier and less stressful to say "I don't know" and move on with your day. Because the truth is you can't know what's going to happen in the future even if you've convinced yourself otherwise.

The only thing you can do is your best and remind yourself that regardless of what happens, you'll survive it.

Focus on the Now

When your thoughts sweep you off your feet and you can't stop agonizing about the past or future, being in the present can break you out of this unhelpful mindset. I know it sounds cliché, but you can't change the past and you have so little control of the future it's laughable. You can only focus on the present moment.

Do this by practicing mindfulness (which will be covered thoroughly in the next chapter) and intently focusing on whatever you're doing at any given time.

Change Your Perspective

Self-talk can be helpful when you need to refresh your opinion of yourself. A great way to do this is by addressing yourself from an outside perspective, so instead of saying, "I feel horrible, but *I* know *I* can get through this," you can say, "I know *you* feel horrible, but *you* can get through this."

What this does is it forces you to look at the situation from a different point of view and be more understanding of your own struggles and intense emotions.

Metacognition

Metacognition is a fancy word that means being aware of your thoughts. It's based on the principle that your thoughts and emotions control your behaviors and actions. Being in control of your mind puts you in charge of your actions.

You can practice being aware of your thoughts by just observing them without judgment or trying to redirect them and then questioning the unhelpful ones (these are usually the persistent negative ones).

This is a common practice in therapy, and it falls under cognitive behavioral therapy (CBT). It's common because it's effective and doesn't require much apart from using logic and critical thinking.

Let me give you an example of how this technique works. You've overslept, and you are definitely going to be late for school. Your initial thought might be that this is a bad way to start the day, and you immediately assume the entire day is ruined just because you overslept.

By using metacognition, you flip the script—accept that you're going to be late for school but at least you'll be there. You stop telling yourself that today is going to suck and try to make the best of the situation anyway. And because you're not assuming that the day is ruined from the start, you can look forward with a fresh outlook instead of attributing every little bad thing that happens to you that day to being late.

When you overthink everything and always assume the worst, you react strongly to every minutely negative thing that happens to you. You missed the bus so obviously the day can only get worse from here. Of course, you forgot your homework at home and stubbed your toe on the stairs, the day was doomed from the start anyway.

One small mistake does not automatically set you up for failure. But it will if you believe so. Your mindset can either drastically improve your day or cause you such misery you wished you never got out of bed in the first place.

ADHD and EFD Explained

People who have autism, ADHD, EFD, traumatic brain injury (TBI), post-traumatic stress disorder (PTSD), along with other neurological disorders are classified as neurodiverse. And the symptoms of all the above mentioned disorders can overlap in certain cases.

For instance, Alzheimer's disease can affect executive function and depression can severely impact working memory, attention, and inhibitions. In addition, sleep deprivation, pain, stress, loneliness, poor health, and substance abuse can even cause otherwise neurotypical individuals to experience impaired executive function.

Executive functioning disorder is not formally recognized as a mental disorder in the DSM-5 (Diagnostics and Statistical Manual of Mental Disorders), but mental health practitioners can determine whether you have problems with executive functioning and suggest treatment options.

Executive Function Disorder

The human brain has seven main executive functions: self-awareness, inhibition, nonverbal working memory, verbal working memory, emotional regulation, motivational regulation, and planning and problem-solving.

Executive function starts to develop at a very young age (from about two years) and is responsible for directing our actions, planning for the future, motivating ourselves, and achieving our goals. Without these critical abilities, it is hard for a person to regulate themselves and follow through with actions and behaviors that might benefit them in the future.

Your memory is mostly saved at the back of your brain, while the front part of your brain (prefrontal cortex) is responsible for interpreting memories that are helpful in the moment. Your prefrontal cortex is where executive functioning mostly takes place, and it has circuits that can answer the four questions: what, when, why, and how?

1. What: This includes working memory, planning, and goals.
2. When: This is responsible for organizing, prioritizing, and timelines.
3. Why: This is in charge of thoughts and feelings.
4. How: This controls self-awareness and past experiences.

When you have executive dysfunction, you might have trouble with one or more of these areas, creating a disconnect. Therefore, you experience symptoms related to memory, planning, emotional regulation, or social skills.

Symptoms of EFD

The symptoms of executive dysfunction are very similar to ADHD. In fact, ADHD is considered to be a more severe form of EFD.

Universal symptoms of EFD include

- **time blindness**: You have trouble gauging how much time has passed.

- **emotional dysregulation**: You take a very long time to calm down or process your feelings, and you act on impulse when you lose your temper.
- **trouble planning ahead**: You struggle with time management and being prepared for events happening in the distant future.
- **information processing difficulties**: You have to reread instructions or ask people to repeat themselves.
- **poor organization:** You can't prioritize important tasks or follow a schedule and have trouble knowing what steps to take to reach your goals.

What Can You Do?

Fortunately, executive functioning is a skill that can be improved with practice and time. There are many different strategies you can use that strengthen your executive functioning.

- Write it out.
- Writing about your struggles not only strengthens your internal monologue and ability to express your feelings but also helps you spot negative thought patterns so you can reframe them.

- You can also make use of prompts that encourage you to rephrase your thinking, such as *three reasons why I shouldn't be worried about that test* or *two reasons why it's okay to make mistakes.*
- Have a goal.
- Think of something easy but specific that you want to accomplish that won't take a long time to do. It could be as simple as saving up some money to buy a video game or getting your driver's license (if you're old enough) as long as the goal is meaningful to you and incentivizes you to follow through with it. Then, once you've managed to successfully plan and follow through, work your way up to more elaborate goals.
- Get a hobby.
- There are many exciting and fun hobbies that exercise self-regulation, such as sports, yoga, singing, playing an instrument, or even playing computer games (as long as you're not spending most of your time on it). These can help engage your attention and improve working memory and reaction times.
- Create a loose schedule.
- If you're having trouble sticking to a daily routine, you can start by doing just one thing every day at around the same time. Doing your homework, for example. Think about when the best time is to do your homework. If you're too tired at night, doing it

as soon as you get home might be a better option. Then try and stick to doing just this one thing on time every day before gradually adding more things to your routine.

ADHD

A person who has ADHD can struggle with multiple executive functions on top of having symptoms of hyperactivity, distractibility, or both.

So, it comes as no surprise that there are three types of ADHD: predominantly inattentive presentation, predominantly hyperactive-impulsive presentation, and a combined presentation.

Predominantly Inattentive Presentation

If you are predominantly inattentive, you may have trouble with organization. This could look like having a messy room, not following a routine or schedule, or being unable to plan or prioritize tasks. You get distracted easily and struggle to follow instructions or pay attention to detail.

You might also struggle to hold a conversation, usually because your mind wanders and you stop listening to the person you're talking to. Though this is usually not done intentionally.

Predominantly Hyperactive-Impulsive

Presentation

If you are predominantly hyperactive or impulsive, you're likely always busy and get restless if you sit still for long periods of time. You're always fidgeting with your hands or bouncing your leg to get rid of some of the pent-up energy. You may talk a lot and interrupt others often.

You are very impatient and get frustrated with waiting in line or waiting your turn. Because of this impulsivity, you might have accidents or injure yourself on a regular basis.

Combined Presentation

If you are having symptoms of both the above mentioned types, you have a combined presentation. This doesn't mean you have all the symptoms of each type, it just means that you fall under both categories somewhat equally.

The thing to remember with ADHD, and most neurological disorders really, is that the symptoms may come and go. You might experience one or more symptoms that's particularly bad today, but tomorrow it's less severe. You could also only have some symptoms. You don't need to have all of the symptoms to be classified as having ADHD.

It's also worth mentioning that your symptoms could change over time, meaning you may move back and forth between these types as you get older.

Labels, Identity, and Mindset

The way you see yourself will play a big role in your ability to overcome challenges related to ADHD and EFD. Take a few minutes to reflect on how you talk to yourself or how you treat yourself. Are you constantly criticizing or minimizing your efforts, telling yourself you can't do something, or putting yourself down?

Treating yourself as "less than" will create a mindset where you believe that you are "less than." You can blame your parents, teacher, and diagnosis all you want, but if you don't take responsibility for yourself, you won't ever grow as a person.

Now, this doesn't mean taking all the blame. But rather understanding your own mind and working around your challenges in order to reach your goals. The ability to adapt to change and use it to improve yourself is called a growth mindset.

However, focusing on your weaknesses and blindly accepting that you're incapable because of your diagnosis creates a victim mentality, which can severely impede personal growth. When a person resists growing as a result of their circumstances, it's called having a fixed mindset.

Obviously, having a growth mindset is preferred because it encourages things like problem-solving, self-education, and building skills and mental abilities. For example, people with a growth mindset believe that you can make any area of your life better or solve any problem with enough time and effort. This greatly improves their chance of succeeding and accomplishing their goals.

Labels and Identity

There's no dispute that ADHD and EFD can severely impact your productivity and daily life. But that doesn't mean you can't achieve greatness. Your diagnosis, or lack thereof, shouldn't have a hold on you. Being neurodiverse is nothing to be ashamed of, and while it is a big part of who you are, it doesn't determine your value in society.

Other people will label you, but your identity remains entirely up to you. So who are you? Think of at least five positive attributes that describe who you are and write them down. Don't include your diagnosis or things other people have said to you. Purely look within yourself and acknowledge who you are as a person.

Maybe you're kind-hearted, thoughtful, creative, funny, dedicated, hardworking, and honest. These are all great traits to have that have nothing to do with your ADHD or EFD. People will try to put you in a box because that's just how society functions. You are capable of so much more than being known as the kid with ADHD.

Advocating for Yourself

Being a teenager isn't easy. You're expected to be responsible and mature even though science tells us that your frontal lobe (the part of the brain responsible for executive functioning) isn't fully developed until the age of 25 (Sharma et al., 2013).

I would argue that being impulsive and taking risks—to a non-life-threatening extent—are important and teach you valuable skills that you might need later on in life. Without these experiences, you can't condition your brain to work correctly, efficiently, or safely.

That being said, impulsivity or being pressured into doing things by your peers are rarely in favor of your well-being. When you do find yourself in a situation where you are being pressured by others or feeling impulsive, it's always advised that you step back and evaluate possible repercussions before you continue.

As an example, I sometimes find myself buying things online that I don't really need on a whim. What I started to do instead is put the item in my cart, but I don't check out. Instead, I'll go back in a few days, or even a week, and think, *do I honestly need this or am I just being impulsive?* Usually, after a few days, I no longer feel the intense desire to have the item, but just the act of adding it to my cart with the intention of buying it later dulled the impulse enough for me to be able to think clearly.

Because ADHD leaves you more sensitive to emotions, both those of others and your own, you might innately be a people pleaser. This might be due to fear of rejection (also called rejection sensitive dysphoria, or RSD) or a higher level of empathy. Regardless, your happiness and comfort should always take priority over expectations that others have set for you.

The difference between being kind and being a people pleaser is pressure. Being kind to others shouldn't feel like a chore or leave you mentally drained. This might be a hot take, but you don't owe people anything just like they don't owe you anything. There's nothing wrong with being kind. In fact, it's a great personality trait to have but not when it comes at the expense of your mental health.

Not being kind doesn't automatically mean you're being rude or insensitive. The thing is, people pleasers have a hard time saying no because they're afraid of disappointing or upsetting others. Therefore, they think being kind means putting immense pressure on themselves to agree with everyone and uphold a perfect image.

If you're always changing your actions or choice of words around others based on what you think they want, avoid conflict at all costs, and find it hard to express your true feelings or say no, you might be a people pleaser. All of your energy is spent making others happy instead of making yourself happy, which can leave you with low self-esteem, feeling pressured by expectations all the time, and susceptible to developing unhelpful coping skills.

Leaving this mindset behind doesn't come easy, and as with most things in life, it will take time, effort, and patience. But ultimately, it's worth it. So here are a few things that could help you overcome your people-pleasing tendencies:

- Be true to yourself.
- Avoid doing anything just because it might improve your image in someone else's mind. Don't change your opinions because someone else disagrees with you, don't try to fit in by acting differently around others, and definitely don't do anything you're not comfortable with.
- Practice saying no more often.
- Don't say "maybe" or "I'll think about it." If you're unsure in any way about anything that's been asked of you, say no. And stop explaining your reasoning behind it. "No" is a complete sentence and not wanting to is a valid reason.
- This does not include responsibilities, unfortunately. It's strictly reserved for when someone asks something of you that's unreasonable. You're not being selfish—you're considering your own feelings.

- Set boundaries.
- The only people who will have a problem with boundaries are the people abusing your people-pleasing nature. Keep that in mind.
- Start by identifying things that other people are doing that make you feel unhappy, uncomfortable, or used. If you're always the one doing all the work in a group project, speak up and stick to your guns. One bad grade won't ruin your life.
- Listen to your gut feeling.
- Throughout your life, there will be people who feel entitled to your efforts and attention but don't offer the same in return. You may find yourself wanting to impress them or have them like you, but listen to your inner voice if it warns you that they might be toxic. This involves getting in touch with yourself and really defining what it is you expect from other people and what you are willing to give (respect, understanding, support, etc.).
- Know it's okay if not everyone likes you.
- This is a hard concept to understand and accept as a people pleaser. You will always be the villain in someone else's story no matter how much good you do or how hard you try to make everyone happy. You are still a good person and likable even if not everyone agrees.
- Ask for help.

- Even if you don't need it, asking for help can be an important step if you're used to being in control of every minute task. It could be as simple as asking a friend for advice or perspective or asking your dad to help rearrange the furniture in your room when the hyperactivity kicks in.
- Accept your imperfections.
- Oftentimes, people pleasers believe that flaws are unacceptable, so they try their best to hide them. I'm not saying you shouldn't try to improve them; however, you can embrace your flaws while also working on improvement. The only opinion that matters should be your own.

Deciding on Medication and Therapy

ADHD is not curable. It's a lifelong disorder and treatment focuses on managing the symptoms so you can function better in your everyday life. If you are on medication, it will need regular evaluation since symptoms can change over time. It is recommended to combine therapy with medications since this is the most effective treatment option (also known as multimodal treatment).

The ultimate goal is to help people who are affected by ADHD and EFD gain the knowledge and tools they need to be able to cope with their disorders and live as much of a normal, healthy lifestyle as possible. This includes building social skills, overcoming learning challenges, and being independent.

Medication

Medications are only prescribed if the symptoms are severe enough to majorly interfere with your ability to learn or develop skills.

These medications work by helping the different parts of the brain work together and communicate to improve executive functioning. They help with symptoms such as inattentiveness, impulsivity, and the inability to finish tasks or prioritize them.

The most commonly prescribed medication for ADHD is methylphenidate (Ritalin and Concerta). But others such as dexamphetamine and lisdexamfetamine (Vyvanse) and "amphetamine" based medications (Adderall, Dexedrine, and DextroStat) can also be prescribed.

However, the only drawback to ADHD medication is the potential side effects that include

- loss of appetite
- reduced height in adulthood (up to 2 cm)
- anxiety or agitation
- insomnia
- dry mouth

- headaches
- upset stomach
- worsening of tics (if you had any before taking the medication)

Bear in mind that if the side effects are persistent and severe, the type, dosage, and timing of medications can be altered to minimize or get rid of them completely. However, your doctor should be monitoring you closely and asking questions about side effects and your ADHD symptoms since starting treatment.

Other medications like atomoxetine and nortriptyline can also help with memory and attention span by encouraging norepinephrine production in the brain. Also, they're less likely to produce adverse side effects.

Therapy

Behavior strategies will be your first line of defense when it comes to managing your ADHD symptoms.

Psychotherapy can help you better understand your symptoms, express your feelings effectively, and learn how to make better choices in the future that benefit you and other people around you.

Behavioral therapy is all about recognizing patterns and gradually changing your responses to internal and external factors that might trigger you. Behavioral therapy also includes cognitive behavioral therapy that aims to break negative or irrational thought patterns and replace them with helpful ones, as well as challenge your beliefs and perspectives.

The bottom line is that it's your decision which route you take, but ultimately, you will have to cope with the sometimes debilitating symptoms of ADHD and EFD through medication, therapy, or better yet, both.

2

MINDFULNESS AND EMOTIONAL REGULATION

Practicing or improving your mindfulness can help calm the symptoms of ADHD since it lowers anxiety and stress levels while also making it easier to identify what you're feeling. When you are aware of what's going on in your body and mind, you can better communicate your needs and express your feelings. This mental skill comes in handy when dealing with responsibilities and social interaction.

Emotional regulation is your ability to deal with your emotions and not let them cloud your judgment or control your actions. Being able to express or process your emotions in a healthy way is key to creating a mindset where you can stay in control of your emotions in a situation where it's necessary to do so.

Mindfulness and emotional regulation are not traits but rather mental skills that can be improved with practice and patience.

Mindfulness

Mindfulness practices include things like meditation and yoga. Though, once you know the basics of how mindfulness works, you can do it at any time when you're completing a mundane task like walking or loading the dishwasher.

Being mindful focuses on the idea of being present and engaged in the moment—it's really as simple as that. It can be done by anyone of any age, and it's extremely effective in reducing stress, anxiety, and even depression (Levine, 2022).

Moreover, it also exercises the prefrontal cortex, which we know is responsible for executive functioning and attentiveness. Practicing mindfulness on a regular basis has the potential to ease or improve symptoms of ADHD in both the short and long term.

Studies show that dedicating just a few minutes a day to practicing mindfulness can improve executive function, attention span, and task initiation while reducing distractibility, hyperactivity, and impulsivity (Greenblatt, 2022).

. . .

HOW TO BE *Mindful*

Mindfulness includes observing your thoughts and identifying your emotions without judgment while engaging yourself fully in whatever you're doing. The idea is to let go of the past and future and simply exist in the now. It can be helpful to tell yourself that you have nothing else to do and nowhere else to be than here and now.

It might take a while to be able to just "switch" your brain to this mindset, but once you do, this ability to take a break—albeit briefly—from your ADHD mind can be extremely calming and refreshing.

Practicing mindfulness doesn't have to be elaborate or time-consuming for it to be effective. There are many strategies and ways to be mindful, so keeping ADHD and EFD in mind, here are some of the simplest ways to be mindful:

- **walking**: Not only is walking great for physical health but also, when paired with mindfulness, it can be beneficial for your mental well-being. While you're walking, focus on your steps and the sensation of the cement, grass, or gravel under your shoes. Notice where your thoughts take you and try to keep them in the present instead of the past or future.

- **listening to music**: You could do this with or without headphones, though, headphones do offer a more immersive experience. With this practice, you simply pick your favorite song and focus on how the song makes you feel. Try to identify sounds or instruments in the background that you might not have noticed before. Alternatively, try to listen to supporting vocals or harmonies in the background.
- **mindful movement**: This ties in with listening to music, just with adding movement. To do this, feel the music and do whatever movements feel right to you. Don't try to make it look good or cohesive—just move your body in tune with the music. This is a great way to express yourself while also getting rid of pent-up emotions or energy.
- **solving puzzles**: Jigsaw puzzles, crosswords, sudoku, spot-the-difference, word searches, riddles, and even board games like chess all fall under this category. Because of the focus, attention to detail, and sometimes strategy required, they can be great exercise for the mind while being fun and engaging. Try to reflect on what you're feeling while participating in it and how it affects your physical body. How does your body respond when you get frustrated, solve the puzzle, or win?
- **download an app**: Having ADHD often means setting dozens of alarms to remind yourself to do

necessary things such as brushing your teeth, taking medication, and taking out the trash. Luckily, there are plenty of mobile apps to choose from that can make keeping track of meditation and mindfulness as easy as possible. Aura, Better Sleep, and Simple Habit are apps geared towards reminding you to do chores, practice mindfulness, and track your mental health.

- **art**: People with ADHD are usually very visual and creative and find great pleasure in expressing themselves in this way. Coloring, drawing, or doodling pairs well with mindfulness exercises while having the added benefit of reward when you've created something you are proud of. The same goes for crafting, painting, and writing.

Emotional Regulation

Emotional regulation does not mean suppressing or ignoring your emotions, nor does it mean reacting intensely to every one of them, but rather regulating the flow of them. Imagine your emotions being like the volume on a powerful speaker; you don't want it muted, but you also don't want it turned up to the max either.

Your perspective plays a larger role in your emotions than you might think. You are a product of your past experiences and memories, and due to this fact, the same situation can cause drastically different reactions in different people.

For example, you may love dark humor, but someone else might get easily offended by it. Your respective mindsets are the biggest contributor to this and the only distinguishable factor involved. It's the same idea with everything else, for example, failing a test might make you feel angry and worthless, while someone else is motivated to study harder because of it.

How to Regulate Your Emotions

First, you need to understand that there's no such thing as a bad emotion. All emotions are equal and valid. Some, like anger and disappointment, might be uncomfortable, but all emotions are there for a reason. Ignoring your body's natural reaction to emotions can be harmful in both the short and long term.

Feeling overwhelmed with emotion at times is normal. Being able to manage or regulate your emotions doesn't mean you never have any or never lose control over them. But having the ability to re-regulate yourself means you can overcome the overwhelm and not have it affect your actions.

Mindfulness is actually very helpful in this aspect because one of the main ways to develop and improve your emotional regulation is the ability to identify what you are feeling and why.

Here are some more exercises that may be helpful when you're building emotional intelligence and working on emotional regulation:

- Reframe your thoughts.
- Assuming and catastrophizing greatly contribute to overreactions and emotional overwhelm. You can reframe by challenging your automatic thoughts.
- Let's say you get called into the principal's office, your immediate thought is you did something wrong or you're in trouble. By the time you get there, you're on the verge of hyperventilating only to find out they just wanted to introduce you to your new tutor. Running with this example, reframing your thoughts could look like asking yourself what evidence you have to back up these thoughts? Did you do something wrong? Is there any reason you're aware of that might justify being called into the principal's office? If not, take deep breaths and try not to assume anything.
- Stop invalidating your feelings.
- Telling yourself things like "It's not that bad," "You're overreacting," and "Just calm down, it's no big deal" even when you are upset over something

seemingly small is unhelpful. Your emotions, even if they are out of proportion, are valid. Accepting all of your emotions—even the ones that are intense or less favorable—will help you get used to them and be more comfortable with them. Eventually, you'll realize that intense emotions are harmless, and it will be easier to handle them.

- Express your emotions in a helpful way at the appropriate time.
- Screaming at your teacher because you are upset that they gave you an "F" on a paper even though you followed every instruction and criterion will only make things worse. This doesn't mean you shouldn't take the matter further or express your frustrations; it just means waiting for the right time.
- For example, you could approach another teacher who teaches the same subject to take a look at it and ask their opinion, then take it up with someone higher up. Next, you want to get out all that anger. You can do this by venting to a friend or parent, punching or screaming into a pillow, or writing a rage-fueled letter and then burning it.
- As long as you're not turning to destroying furniture or hurting others or yourself (physically or mentally), there's no wrong way to express your anger.
- Distract yourself temporarily.

- When you find yourself in a situation where you are feeling overwhelmed with anger or any other intense emotion, distracting yourself until you're calm enough to deal with the situation can be helpful. The key word here is "temporarily." You should always revisit the problem and try to work on solving the conflict rather than avoiding it. This could look like going for a walk, watching a funny video, or talking to a non-biased person about it.

Self-Control and Self-Regulation

In psychology, self-control theory focuses on the reasons why you might keep yourself from participating in behaviors that are potentially unhealthy or dangerous or that hinder a future goal.

If you want to buy an entire gaming setup, you first have to save up for it. Thus, you have to resist the urge to spend money. Getting involved with the wrong crowd that abuses alcohol or other drugs could lead you to use it yourself, which is not only unhealthy but also potentially life-ruining. Regardless of your motives for choosing not to indulge, whether it's consequence or reward, it's the driving force behind self-control.

Since we're only human, we sometimes give in to these temptations. You use some of your savings on a whim to buy a new trending gadget, or you don't want to be the only one not drinking at a party because you fear being ridiculed by others.

However, there's value in knowing which areas you lack self-control. When you know where you're lacking impulse control, you can work on building it so you're less likely to give in when these scenarios inevitably occur in the future.

The elements that make up self-control theory are the ability to defer gratification, the ability to be cautious, and cognitive abilities, such as reading, thinking, attention, and memory.

Why do we give in to temptation? Because of gratification. Our brains want to be rewarded, and unfortunately, most behaviors that have instant gratification are unhealthy or unhelpful in the long run. Doing drugs, buying something frivolous, sleeping in instead of exercising, having fast food every day, and so on. All these actions have one thing in common—they release a feel-good hormone that gives you an incentive to continue doing it.

Deferring gratification means you can weigh the short-term with the long-term effect or outcome and rule in favor of the most beneficial one. It might not be easy to get up earlier every day and exercise for 30 minutes, but it's good for you and helps reduce your anxiety and other ADHD symptoms. Alternatively, you could distract yourself from the instant gratification you'll get. For example, tell yourself that if you still want the trendy gadget by the end of the week, you'll get it then.

Furthermore, the ability to be cautious is an obvious element, but it's one that's still very important for self-control. Being paranoid or anxious about the potential risks involved in your decisions is a good thing when these behaviors are not inherently beneficial.

Cognitive abilities include thinking, reading, learning, memory, and attention. All these mental skills make it possible for you to solve problems, overcome obstacles and challenges, grow and evolve intellectually, and conquer your goals. Many things may contribute to your inability to control your impulses or desires, which is why it's important to strengthen your cognitive skills. Doing something without a second thought is almost never a good idea.

Another subcategory of cognitive abilities is emotional intelligence. Emotional intelligence is the ability to be objective and consider different perspectives when it comes to managing your emotions and resolving conflict, whether that conflict is internal or external. When you have well-developed emotional intelligence, you are better able to regulate your emotions in difficult situations—like turning the volume up or down as discussed earlier.

. . .

Improving Self-Control

Now that you're more familiar with what self-control is, you're probably wondering what you can do to work on it or improve it. Whether you're spending too much time on Netflix, struggling with sticking to a routine, or putting off an assignment until the night before it's due, strengthening your self-control and self-regulatory skills can help you be more productive.

Self-control is important for many reasons. When you are capable of prioritizing long-term goals over short-term pleasures, you feel more in control of your life and are more satisfied with your accomplishments. Research shows that people who have strong self-control are more likely to be healthy, successful, and have better relationships (Stafford, 2011).

There are a few strategies you can resort to when you find yourself in a situation where it is difficult for you to resist temptation. Remember that the aim is improvement through practice and not perfection. Self-control is no different than any other skill—the more you do it, the better you get at it.

- **healthy distractions**: You have a limited amount of self-control, but by utilizing distractions, you override this limitation. The longer you resist the urge, the weaker your resolve gets. Distracting yourself stops this from happening. Healthy distractions include things like playing with your dog, calling a friend, cleaning your room, getting started on an assignment, exercising, or participating in any of your creative hobbies. Chances are, your ADHD will cause you to forget what you wanted in the first place (that's a joke).

- **plan for temptation**: Temptations that hinder us from achieving our goals are all around us and nearly impossible to avoid. So the next logical step is to plan. Think about what you could do the next time you encounter temptations that are hard for you to resist. Let's say you're avoiding sugar because you discovered it makes you break out but it's your friend's birthday. You still want to go to the party to show your support and offer your congratulations, but obviously, there will be cake. One option could be to eat a well-balanced, fiber- and protein-rich breakfast before you go to avoid hunger pains making it more difficult to resist a slice of cake. Then, inform your friend that you will regrettably not be having a piece of dessert.

- **focus on one area at a time**: If you have multiple areas where you lack self-control, taking them all on at once will overwhelm you. Instead, pick one to start with before moving on to the next one.

- **meditation**: Meditation can improve your overall self-control by bringing awareness to the mind and body and slowing down thoughts and impulses. The act of meditating in itself requires a fair amount of self-discipline, which will further contribute to mental and physical control.

Don't be too hard on yourself if and when you fail to resist any or all temptations. As long as you're making an effort, you will eventually get to a place where practicing self-control comes easy.

Inhibitory Control and Responsive Inhibition

Inhibition is the thing that's holding you back from doing or saying what you want because of consequences. It's driven by fear and anxiety, which isn't necessarily a bad thing if it's proportionate and keeps you out of harm's way. It encourages you to be careful around strangers and in potentially dangerous situations, for example.

Cognitive Inhibition

Inhibitory control is more commonly known as selective attention, or the ability to ignore irrelevant stimuli or interference. Most of the time there is always something happening around you and being able to tune it out or not be distracted by it is important.

When you are trying to study for a test but all you can focus on is the construction noises from the roadworks being completed down the street, the sound of dishes clashing together from your mom cleaning the kitchen, and the ticking of the clock feels like it's mounted on the inside of your skull, you might have troubles with inhibitory control.

The inability to block out certain distractions and focus on what is necessary is commonly identified in people with ADHD.

Behavioral Inhibition

Behavioral inhibition encapsulates the same idea as cognitive inhibitions, just relating to behaviors and actions. It could also be classified as part of self-control since it involves resisting strong urges and patience when it comes to receiving gratification.

A prime example of a behavioral inhibition that is taught to kids from a young age is the ability to wait their turn and wait to speak or give an answer instead of interrupting someone mid-sentence or blurting something out in class.

Granted, with ADHD, the urge to interrupt someone to say something might have something to do with memory in the sense that you are afraid you might forget what you were going to say.

Improving Inhibitory Control and Responsive Inhibition

Inhibition is also part of executive function. Since they're so closely related, improving general executive functioning should, in theory, improve inhibitory control. Regardless, if you want a more head-on approach, feel free to try out the following strategies to improve inhibitions:

- **physical activity**: This includes any type of physical activity, it could be dancing, swimming, boxing, gymnastics, or even just walking. Try to get at least 30 minutes of physical activity in most days of the week.
- **task switching**: Pick two things on your to-do list that are both relatively easy and quick to complete (for example, raking leaves and folding laundry) and do them back-to-back without taking a break. Alternatively, you could choose two tasks that are similar to each other (doing homework and proofreading an assignment) and combine them. Someone with ADHD is more likely to be able to multitask since their shortened attention span makes it impossible to focus on one thing at a time, though this is not always the case.
- **video games**: Studies show that playing certain types of video games (mainly role-playing and

action-based games) can improve cognitive and executive functioning skills since they rely on problem-solving, overcoming challenges, working memory, perspective, and attention to detail (Gysi, 2016). However, you should still limit how much time you spend playing video games and take regular breaks.

3

HABITS AND ORGANIZATION

Adopting habits that make your life easier is, without a doubt, a good thing to do. However, when you have ADHD or EFD, forming habits is 10 times harder than it is for someone who doesn't have these disorders.

If you view habit forming and organization as skills that can be improved and mastered, they get less intimidating.

Good habits and organizational skills are essential to have since they are crucial for completing goals and staying on top of what needs to be done every day for you to achieve the accomplishments you set out for yourself.

Habits

By definition, a habit is a learned behavior that is regularly repeated and doesn't take much thought or effort to remember.

However, if you have ADHD or EFD, you should know right off the bat that that definition does not apply to you. A habit is learned behavior, that fact still applies, but the "not much effort" part is completely misleading.

You will most likely have to set a reminder for a very long time, if not indefinitely, before the action becomes automatic or part of your routine. Forming new habits is also a great way to continue practicing inhibitory control.

First off, there are a few habits that will help you manage or decrease the severity of your ADHD or EFD symptoms. I would recommend starting on these since everything else becomes so much easier when you're not overwhelmed with life.

Habits that might help lessen symptoms of ADHD and EFD include

- **getting enough sleep**: Giving your brain a time-out from reality is crucial to mental and physical health. You need a minimum of eight hours of sleep every day. It's important that this is quality sleep, meaning uninterrupted, blissful sleep. This is hard to ensure since you can't help it if you keep waking up at night. A bedtime routine can help, and it doesn't have to be elaborate or lengthy. Though, if your sleeping pattern is regularly interrupted, I urge you to see a doctor that might be able to prescribe something that helps with this.

- **managing stress**: With everything you need to remember to do every day, simplifying your life as much as possible can help reduce overwhelm. Cut down on activities or commitments that don't serve you and drain your mental or social battery (such as clubs, gatherings, or extracurricular activities that don't interest you). Also, try out a few relaxation techniques or activities and continue with the one that's most helpful. This could be anything that brings you peace and calmness (a hot shower, bubble bath, reading a book, meditation or deep breathing, listening to music, etc.)

- **using a system to manage tasks**: When you have ADHD or EFD, everything might seem equally important to you, meaning you have trouble organizing in which order things should be done. Implementing an uncomplicated system to keep track of everything you need to do can be helpful. Once everything is written down randomly, you can then divide them into categories, such as things to remember," "things to do," and "project list." It's pretty self-explanatory, but everything that requires more than two steps should go on the project list. For example, taking out the trash can go on the "things to do" list, but writing a school paper should go on the "project list" because it includes research, writing, sourcing, editing, proofreading, and submitting. Once you've broken down all the necessary steps to complete a project, put one or two steps on your "things to do" list at a time.

- **being proud of your accomplishments**: Silence the "would've, could've, should've" voices by reminding yourself of everything you did manage to do today, even if the only thing you managed to get done was get out of bed.

- **trying even when it's hard**: Don't expect to always succeed. There will be days when you forget or don't have the mental capacity to do something. Just don't lose hope and disregard all your progress because of a bad day. You can always try again tomorrow after a good night's rest, and if tomorrow is also bad, you repeat the process until you eventually get where you want to be.

Getting Habits to Stick

A healthy habit is a behavior that is repeated often or daily that benefits your mental and physical health. This includes eating as healthy as possible, getting at least 30 minutes of exercise a day, staying hydrated, getting enough sleep, and so on.

Though, there are many other habits that you can include in your daily routine that will make it easier to stay on top of things while also improving executive function and other mental skills, the problem usually lies in getting the habit to stick.

You may lack the motivation or energy to keep going and repeat the same behavior every day. The repetitiveness becomes boring, and you end up just forgetting about it or not caring enough to continue.

Knowing what you can and can't control and accepting it are powerful mindsets. You have ADHD or EFD, which makes it extremely hard to stick to a routine or form a habit. You can't control it, but you can choose to not feel guilty about it and to keep trying no matter how many times you might fail.

Resist the urge to change everything at once. The best approach is always small steps, and while it might take longer, you're more likely to succeed when you make small changes that are manageable instead of taking leaps and bounds.

Plan ahead for moments of weakness. Once you've added a new habit to your schedule and you've done it consistently for a few days, spend some time evaluating what about this new habit could make you want to quit or what might make it hard to keep doing it. Then, brainstorm a few ways you can make it easier or more rewarding to ensure you stay on track. Play around with the time of day you're doing it, find ways to simplify it, or link it to other habits you might already have.

Track your progress and reward yourself. This could be something like making a little cross on the calendar date if you've done the activity or task that you're trying to make a habit of or journaling your thoughts and experiences with the activity every day. Don't forget to reward yourself when you do manage to complete the habit for the day. This could be something like having a family movie night or playing your favorite video game for an hour or two without feeling guilty.

Having someone who can help keep you accountable could also be something that might help you stay on track even if you don't have the motivation to do so. This could be a friend, a sibling, or even a supportive parent.

Organization

You might be part of the minority of people who have ADHD or EFD but do not struggle with organizing, prioritizing, and planning, but for the majority of people with ADHD, this is a persistent and debilitating issue.

The ability to plan, prioritize, and organize your thoughts as well as your environment is essential to finish tasks, reach your goals, and be productive. The goal here is not to plan or organize your entire life perfectly but rather to create a balance between your school and home life so you don't feel so lost all the time.

Constantly losing homework and assignments and missing deadlines can contribute to unnecessary stress and poor grades even though you're an extremely intelligent and creative person. And even if you only manage to transform chaos into a general mess, it's still a step forward and something you should be proud of.

Organization is personal and unique to everyone based on their problems and struggles. There are many different systems that consult different aspects of organization. You may struggle with organizing time but not tasks, or you are good at organizing things but not time. Whichever is giving you a hard time, there are things you can do to overcome it.

Organizing Time

If you are someone who tackles a school project the night before it's due because you either forgot about it or misjudged the amount of time you had left to complete it, you might have trouble organizing time.

The biggest mistake someone with ADHD can make is to tell themselves, "I don't have to write that down, I'll remember." You're constantly forgetting why you entered a room, but you convince yourself you'll remember something you need to do three weeks from now?

There's nothing wrong with needing some help. In fact, I encourage you to find as many shortcuts and loopholes that "hack" your ADHD as you can. Need to remember to take something with you when you leave the house, and it doesn't fit in your bag? Place it right in front of the door. You'll have to move it to open the door, so you'll see it and remember you need to take it.

Planning your time doesn't mean you have to plan out every waking hour; in fact, doing so will likely result in failure, leaving you feeling frustrated and discouraged. Only plan out the important tasks and leave the rest empty to give yourself the flexibility to take breaks and to anticipate unexpected or unplanned activities or tasks.

Most smartphones have a built-in calendar system that allows you to create a schedule, and as a bonus, they usually come with reminders that pop up on screen. Start by adding in one or two things that you should be doing every day but usually forget, such as brushing your teeth.

Another aspect that might make time management difficult if you have ADHD or EFD is underestimating how much time it will take to complete the project. It's always better to over-compensate than fall behind schedule. A good rule to have is taking the time that you think it's going to take to finish a certain project or task and multiplying it by 1.5, meaning if you think it's going to take you an hour, assume that it's going to take an hour and a half.

Organizing Tasks

Let's say you're fairly good at managing time, but you still struggle to meet deadlines or finish everything on your to-do list because you have trouble determining which tasks are most important. To you, writing a 1,000-word essay might feel just as important and take just as much mental energy as loading the dishwasher.

In this scenario, the best way to judge the importance of a task is to gauge the possible consequences if you don't do it. If you forget to load the dishwasher or make your bed, your mom might remind you to do it or express her frustrations. On the other hand, if you don't hand in your essay tomorrow, you risk it reflecting badly on your grades. Therefore, the essay is more important at that moment.

If you get easily overwhelmed with tasks that require multiple steps, you could use the same strategy discussed in the previous heading where you break down a task that has multiple steps into smaller, more manageable tasks. Let's use the essay again as an example. It's due tomorrow, but you haven't even picked a topic yet. Since that's the logical first step, you can start there. But it also includes many other things to take into consideration: research, planning (with a mind map or writing down points of discussion), proofreading and editing, and then the final draft. By focusing on each of these tasks as if they were separate, you can avoid becoming overwhelmed.

If you're unsure of which topic to pick, start by writing down a few talking points under each topic and choose the one that has the most. This will ensure you don't run out of things to discuss halfway through. Then move on to the next step that is to research the topic thoroughly and add talking points to your existing list before creating a mind map and organizing the discussions in a way that makes sense. Work your way down the list of things that need to be done for the essay to be completed and before you know it you're done.

By separating the individual steps to a larger project, you can focus on one thing at a time. This way you don't try to complete everything at once and end up feeling mentally and emotionally drained with nothing to show for it.

Organizing Things

When you have ADHD, the phrase "out of sight, out of mind" rings very true. Have you ever deep cleaned your room and found items you forgot you even had because they were at the back of your closet, sealed in a box? This can happen with people who don't have ADHD, but it's way more intense for people with ADHD because it happens so quickly. Homework you had just gotten today stops existing to you because you can't see it in your backpack.

This is partially due to object permanency, which starts to develop in early childhood. A baby may start crying when he doesn't see his mom because he thinks that if he doesn't see her, she doesn't exist. If you have ADHD and you struggle with remembering things, especially relating to objects and things you need to do, this could be because of a deficit with object permanence. What's interesting is it can even extend to people. You may know they still exist, but you find yourself going weeks or months without thinking of them unless you're seeing them on a regular basis.

Having a designated spot for important things and paper-work, such as homework and permission slips, may help with this, but it can also become cluttered quickly if you don't stay on top of sorting through them. It's also important that these things are visible. Use open trays or see-through plastic envelopes.

Minimize clutter. Store away sentimental items to prevent them from getting lost or damaged and get rid of (or donate) anything that you haven't used in a year. If you don't have enough space to give something a permanent spot where it can stay, it should either be thrown out, donated, or put in long-term storage, such as the basement, attic, garage, or any other type of storage option. Under your bed is not a permanent storage solution!

Try to use open shelving or bookcases to store items or objects (in clear storage containers) so they're within plain sight but not cluttering up your room or desk space.

Clutter can definitely contribute to feelings of anxiety and overwhelm. Your room doesn't have to be spotless but minimizing the amount of stuff that's in your way can help you focus on the things you need to remember.

I find that most people with ADHD have a love-hate relationship with routines and schedules. On the one hand, they find it painfully repetitive and restricting, but on the other hand, they feel like it's needed to keep them accountable because, otherwise, they end up wasting so much time being unproductive.

My advice is to apply the 80/20 principle. The 80/20 rule (otherwise known as the Pareto principle) states that 20% of your effort makes up 80% of the results. There are many ways to interpret this rule, but the most important thing is knowing which 20% you should focus your efforts on.

The Pareto principle is usually applied in work or school situations, but it could also be helpful in your personal life. For example, from a business perspective, 80% of sales come from 20% of your marketing efforts, so the goal is to figure out which marketing tactics are most efficient and focus on those.

From a student attending school's perspective, 80% of your project results will come from 20% of the effort you put in. Again, the goal is to figure out which tasks or efforts to prioritize. Though, this is highly specific to the project or assignment at hand. Assignments or projects typically have a rubric that outlines the criteria the project will be graded on. This could be useful to determine where you want to focus your attention.

With regard to utilizing it on a personal level, the rule remains the same. Eighty percent of your problems are caused by twenty percent of issues. In this case, it's likely your ADHD and the symptoms associated with it that are making your life feel impossibly difficult. So addressing them should be priority number one.

Working Memory

Working memory is also known as short-term memory. It's where your brain stores information while it's being processed and is then moved to long-term memory. Working memory involves reordering (rearranging data); updating (constant monitoring of new information and replacing outdated ones); and dual processing (the ability to absorb and retain information while focusing on a task).

Studies show that as much as 85% of people who have ADHD struggle with working memory, which is important for academic achievement, organization, emotion processing, and maintenance of social relationships.

You use working memory for things such as remembering what's on your to-do list, following multistep instructions, comprehending reading and math, and following conversations.

However, it doesn't end there. Long-term memory can also suffer under the guise of ADHD and poor working memory since long-term memory depends so much on working memory to process and store information in a way that makes sense. When information is stored disorderly by working memory, long-term memory won't be able to hold on to it because it deems the information useless or confusing.

While ADHD does affect memory, no evidence suggests that ADHD causes memory loss. It's more a case of your brain never processing the information correctly or fully to begin with rather than losing chunks of existing memory.

Working memory and memory retention are closely related to the severity of your ADHD symptoms. On a bad day, your working memory will be worse than on a good day. It also means by reducing or managing your symptoms, your memory will automatically improve with time.

Improving Working Memory

Forgetfulness can complicate your life drastically. As a teenager, your academics can suffer because of missed deadlines, forgotten homework, inattentiveness while studying, and procrastination. But as an adult, the repercussions are way more severe than an "F" on your report card. Late payments lead to fines and missed payments can cause your internet or power to be shut off or your car to be repossessed and can even get you into some legal trouble.

This is why it's a good idea to improve your memory now while the consequences are a mere slap on the wrist.

So how do you work on improving your memory?

- **medication**: If your working memory is so bad it interferes with your quality of life it might be worth it to try going on medication that might help not only decrease ADHD symptoms but also improve memory troubles.
- **organization tools**: Make use of mobile apps, lists, alarms, reminders, calendars, post-it notes, diaries, etc. to help keep track of important things on your schedule or to-do list.

- **games**: Games that focus on concentration, matching, and planning can be great for working memory. Keep in mind that playing these games all day is also not great for productivity, so aim to limit the time you spend playing games that improve memory.
- **repetition**: The more you practice or do the thing you want to remember, the more easily you will remember it. Repeating or rehearsing information or tasks will help solidify them into your daily routine.

4

HEALTH

Mental and physical health are closely related, and one can dramatically impact the other. So, it's critical that you see both your mental and physical well-being as equally important because they are.

Think back to the last time you had the flu and how it impacted you mentally. The physical symptoms like a sore throat, fatigue, body aches, and fever understandably dampened your mood as well. Furthermore, when you suffer from mental disorders such as anxiety, stress, and depression, they can manifest into physical symptoms, like chest pain, dizziness, headaches, high blood pressure, etc.

By taking care of your physical and mental health, you will feel better, have more energy and confidence, and, therefore, be better equipped to manage symptoms of ADHD and EFD. So how do you take care of yourself both physically and mentally?

Self-Care

I think most people don't really know how to take care of themselves because it's not something that's taught. Sure, you know that eating healthy and working out are good for your health, but self-care is about much more than just that.

Self-care is about prioritizing tasks and activities that benefit you both in the short and long term. It includes physical, emotional, psychological, spiritual, and social care (Franklin, 2017).

- **physical self-care**: Take care of your physical body to the best of your ability. This means eating a healthy diet, getting regular exercise, wearing the clothes you like, doing your hair the way you like, sleeping enough, and taking breaks when you feel you need to.
- **emotional self-care**: Accepting your emotions without shame or judgment either from others or yourself is important. Whatever emotions you have are valid, regardless of other people's opinions. Taking care of your emotional needs includes

allowing yourself to experience whatever emotions you are feeling, using positive self-talk and daily affirmations, and expressing your emotions without fear.

- **psychological self-care**: Setting boundaries with regard to the amount of energy you have to give to others can be a powerful way to take care of your psychological health. Practice saying no to activities or things that don't benefit you and just deplete your energy. Expand your area of expertise and interests, allow yourself to be curious, reflect on your own opinions and thought patterns, pay attention to your inner experiences, challenge your beliefs and assumptions, and acknowledge your worth and value.

- **spiritual self-care**: Whether you believe in a higher power or not, spiritual self-care can be utilized. Religion can absolutely be part of your spirituality if it helps you, but in this case, it's more about getting in touch with your soul and who you are as a person. You can practice spiritual self-care by taking part in a cause you believe in (volunteering or donating to charity), meditating, being surrounded by nature, appreciating the non-materialistic aspects of life, watching or reading inspirational material, and, of course, praying, if you are religious.

- **social care**: Maintaining a balance between your personal life and your school work, or once you enter the workforce, the balance between home and work life, is essential. This includes getting to know your peers (or colleagues) and your teachers (or bosses), managing your workload so you don't become overwhelmed, having a hobby, and creating a designated space to complete homework (or work assignments).

Ideally, you want to include at least one activity from each category and make it part of your daily routine. For example, besides taking care of your physical health (sleeping, eating, and exercising), you can write down daily affirmations; spend as much time as you can afford working on your hobby, reading, or playing video games; and do a quick mindfulness exercise before bed. Also, practice saying no when other people ask things of you if you don't have the capacity to do it.

Self-Care for ADHD

People who have ADHD or EFD often feel like there's not enough time in a day to do everything on their schedules. While everyone feels this way sometimes, people who don't have ADHD or EFD find it easier to prioritize and plan accordingly during times of high stress or pressure.

Because of this, self-care for people with ADHD and EFD might look a bit different. All the categories should still be ticked; however, practicing self-care some of the time is still better than not practicing it at all.

The goal is to build up to a place where you are implementing enough self-care that it's benefiting your productivity and energy levels, and then gradually increase or add activities and tasks while monitoring your level of overwhelm.

If you try to change everything about your lifestyle and add all the activities at the same time, you are almost guaranteed to fail. The ability to stay consistent with your efforts is the most important.

Here are a few self-care tips and strategies that might help you regain peace and power over your mind as well as tone down symptoms of ADHD (Peterson, n.d.):

- You aren't ADHD, you have ADHD.
- While you'll have to live with ADHD for the rest of your life, it doesn't have to define who you are as a person. Living with ADHD or EFD can be extremely debilitating, but it doesn't make you less than worthy.
- Make a list of everything that frustrates you about yourself. Maybe it's the fact that you're always late, always forgetting something, always misplacing

something, disassociating in the middle of a conversation, you're always tired, etc. Then, compare the list to the symptoms of ADHD or EFD and highlight the ones that correlate.

- You'll find that most of the things on the list of things that frustrate you are actually symptoms of ADHD or EFD. They're not character flaws— they're symptoms.
- Now, make a list of all the things you like about yourself or of everything you excel at despite your ADHD or EFD. Maybe your intuition is always on point; you're extremely creative or innovative; you're funny, honest, kind, empathetic, caring, hard-working, knowledgeable, passionate, etc.
- There is so much more to who you are as a person than having ADHD or EFD.
- Do a bodily check-in.
- People with ADHD have a hard time being able to define and pinpoint their emotions. You might not notice when your body is trying to tell you something. This includes things like not knowing when you're hungry, thirsty, or just need a break until you're at the point of burnout.
- Try to check in with yourself throughout the day and ask yourself questions such as: How am I feeling? Did I have lunch today? How much water

have I had today? How long have I been busy with this task? When was the last time I took a break?

- Simply gauge how you're feeling and act accordingly. It might take some time before you can immediately identify what you're feeling or what you need, but the more you do it the easier it gets.
- Engage your senses.
- Engaging your senses might stimulate your brain in a way that makes it easier for you to concentrate. You'll need to experiment with different stimuli before you discover what works for you. Also, don't try to engage all your senses at once since this might be more distracting or overwhelming.
- You can do this by lighting a scented candle; listening to some nature-derived sounds, soothing music, or white or brown noises (easily accessible on YouTube); dimming the lights; adjusting the air conditioning to a temperature you find comfortable; etc. Play around with them separately or together until you find a combination that aids you while studying, doing homework, or working on a project.
- Make loose routines.
- Your brain craves stability and predictability, and a routine provides this. Work on creating a general routine for things like studying, going to bed, getting ready for school, etc. Write it down because you will forget.

- Don't put too much pressure on yourself to follow the routines perfectly or even in order—just use it as a guideline.
- An example of a routine for when you get ready in the morning is: eat breakfast, brush teeth, get dressed, make sure everything is in your bag (write down a general checklist for everyday use) and leave for school. Most of these can be shuffled around, but the idea is to have all the basics written down, so you don't forget anything.
- Know yourself.
- Your preferences, past experiences, interests, strengths, weaknesses, and specific ADHD symptoms should be taken into consideration for your lifestyle and routines. These should be personalized based on what works best for you. If you prefer doing your homework at night because you have a burst of energy around sunset, then that's when you should study.
- Exercise.
- No one likes it, but exercise is essential, especially since it can reduce hyperactivity and mind clutter and release hormones and endorphins that stabilize symptoms of ADHD and EFD. It doesn't even have to be structured exercise. As little as 30 minutes of exercise is enough to receive the benefits. You could take the dog for a walk or do

some stretching or yoga in the comfort of your
bedroom.

- Ask for support when you need it.
- Self-care is also recognizing when you need help
  and asking for it. There's nothing wrong with asking
  people who care about you for support, whether it
  be physical or emotional. They'll most likely be
  happy to help.
- Alternatively, you can practice openly
  communicating with your family members about the
  struggles you face every day and brainstorm ways
  that they can help make it easier on you.
- Find purpose and meaning.
- The irony of having ADHD is you crave stability
  and predictability; however, you also get bored very
  easily. This leads to mundane—yet important—
  activities becoming unbearable to do. You can try to
  adjust or change up your routine often and change
  the way you do these things or think of boring tasks
  as side quests in the game of life. But ultimately, it's
  best to evaluate long-term goals often and remind
  yourself why you're doing what you're doing
  every day.

Exercise

Any activity that gets your heart rate up and your body moving is considered exercise. There are many compelling reasons why you should include at least 30 minutes of exercise in your daily routine—it improves blood circulation, brain function, oxygenation, quality of sleep, metabolism, and self-esteem. It also reduces stress, anxiety, and the risk of heart disease and stroke.

But besides all that, regular exercise can help manage symptoms of ADHD and EFD because it increases the amount of dopamine, scrotonin, and norepinephrine released in the brain. And as we know, ADHD is largely the result of an inconsistent or lack of production of these specific hormones (Oscar-Berman et al., 2008).

Aerobic exercise (or cardio) is the most effective exercise for people with ADHD since these exercises maximize the amount of hormones and endorphins produced and released in the brain. However, there are still some benefits to calming exercises, such as yoga and stretching, since they slow down the mind.

Many people with ADHD say that it feels like there's constant buzzing in their heads as if multiple internal monologues and streams of consciousness are playing over each other. It's no wonder you're exhausted all the time.

Exercise can help combat this by quieting the buzzing in your mind so you can focus on one thing at a time instead of being overwhelmed and overstimulated. As a result, you can concentrate better and for longer periods.

There are many online resources for simple exercise routines. However, your workout routine doesn't have to be structured at all. It could also just form part of your daily activities. For example, you can opt to cycle or walk to or from school instead of taking the bus (that's assuming the school isn't too far from home). Or you could spend 10 minutes stretching in the mornings or before bed at night.

The best exercise routine will always be the one that fits your preference and lifestyle. If it's an inconvenience to you, it's not going to work out in the long term. Luckily, there's no rule to creating your own schedule. You could split up the 30 minutes of physical activity and do 10 minutes, 3 times a day, or 15 minutes, 2 times a day. Furthermore, you could do cardio exercises for the first 15 minutes, and then later in the day you can do stretches or yoga for the other 15 minutes, and so on. This provides variety and reduces the chances of you getting bored with your routine.

If you feel like 30 minutes a day is too much, start with just 10 minutes of exercise. Any effort is still better than none at all. After a while, your body will become used to doing some type of exercise every day, and then you can increase the amount of time you spend exercising a day by five minutes. Eventually, you will get to a point where doing some type of workout for 30 minutes a day is the norm.

I also think it's worth mentioning that there will be days when you don't feel like working out at all. It's okay to skip a day here and there, or even multiple days in a row. As long as you hold on to the mentality that you're not giving up and you still plan on getting back into it, there's no harm done. There's no need to shame or guilt yourself into sticking to a workout plan. Just try and keep to it the majority of the time and you'll still experience the benefits of it.

Certain hobbies can also count as exercise, which is great news for someone with ADHD since you get the physical and mental benefits of exercise while also learning or practicing a skill that they find fun. Hobbies that also count as exercise include

- dancing
- roller skating or ice skating
- building or crafting
- cooking or baking
- foraging
- rock climbing
- swimming
- playing with your pet
- playing an instrument

Nutrition

You've most likely at some point heard the term "you are what you eat." As cliché as it might seem, it's true to a degree. Everything you put in your body gets digested and used as fuel or for regenerative purposes. Sugar, carbohydrates, and oil mainly supply you with energy whereas protein is used as building blocks to create new tissue, muscle, or hair and to manage metabolism in addition to giving you energy.

A healthy diet can help reduce the symptoms of ADHD and EFD because certain foods can interfere with or affect our mood, behaviors, and alertness. Nutrient deficiencies can also worsen the symptoms of ADHD and EFD, which is why a balanced diet that contains all the necessary vitamins and minerals is essential.

However, committing to a healthy, balanced diet doesn't mean cutting out all the foods that you enjoy. It's about creating a balance and eating as healthy as possible whenever you can.

What Is a Healthy Diet?

A healthy diet supplies the body with enough macro- and micronutrients, as well as vitamins, minerals, and fiber, to maintain overall health. As a general rule of thumb, a healthy diet includes

- fresh fruits
- vegetables
- whole grains
- healthy fats
- low-fat dairy products
- lean meat, poultry, and fish
- beans and legumes
- eggs
- seeds and nuts

There's a lot to be said about basal metabolic rates and portion sizes; however, for a developing child or adolescent, intuitive eating should be practiced. Intuitive eating is when you listen to your body and eat only until you're satisfied and not until you're full or because it tastes good.

Portion sizes will provide you with a general guideline on how much you should be putting on your plate to avoid overeating. Every meal should include a source of protein, carbohydrates, fruit or vegetables, and healthy fats.

An ideal meal on a plate should consist of a quarter plate of protein, another quarter should be carbohydrates, and half of your plate should be fruits or vegetables that are high in fiber.

For instance, a healthy breakfast can be a bowl of high-fiber cereal with low-fat milk, plus a small bowl of mixed berries. Lunch can be a peanut butter sandwich with an apple, and dinner can be baked vegetables with mashed potatoes and chicken filets. Snacks can be enjoyed throughout the day or in-between mealtimes and can include things like a handful of nuts between breakfast and lunch, a banana between lunch and dinner, and a few crackers and cheese before bed.

If you have a sweet tooth and you can't see yourself giving up things like chocolate or candy, you don't have to. But try to avoid making it a daily occurrence. Having a few scoops of ice cream, a small bag of chips, or a few blocks of chocolate as a snack between meals a few days a week is perfectly okay, but don't replace an entire meal with it or overdo it. Indulging in your beloved sugary or salty snacks can still form part of an overall healthy diet as long as you remember that they should be treated as snacks and not meals.

Foods to Avoid

Now that we know food and nutrition affects behavior and, therefore, ADHD symptoms, we can start paying closer attention to what we put into our body. The way nutrition affects you might be different from how it does someone else, so you'll most likely need to do a lot of experimentation and elimination before you can know which foods influence your ADHD in which ways.

But first, there are some foods and drinks that you should try to avoid regardless since they have been proven to worsen symptoms of ADHD and EFD. These include caffeine and alcohol.

Seeing as this book is aimed at children and teenagers, you shouldn't be consuming alcohol anyway. Not only can alcohol stunt your development and change the chemistry in your brain permanently, but it also affects your behavior and ADHD symptoms for the worse. I know it can be tempting to try the forbidden fruit, but it's honestly not worth it. In my experience, all it does is bring out the worst in people and make them irresponsible, and it could also lead to addiction and other mental and physical health issues.

Coffee is a stimulant and, to many people, a necessary start to the day. It works by increasing the amount of adrenalin that's released into your system. Although coffee might help with concentration and alertness in people with ADHD, it can also increase feelings of stress and anxiety, which might inherently cancel out the possible benefits of concentration and focus. Also, many people who have ADHD actually report feeling more tired after having coffee.

A healthy alternative to coffee is green tea. It still contains caffeine along with theanine, which actually helps reduce anxiety. I guess the only possible downside would be the taste since not everyone is a fan of green tea.

Caffeine can also be found in things like chocolate, soda, energy drinks, and even some fruits and vegetables.

There are many contradicting studies on whether or not sugar worsens the symptoms of ADHD. So, you might want to add sugar to your elimination list and see for yourself if it's making your symptoms worse or not.

Elimination Diet List

A food elimination list is an experiment of sorts to help you discover which foods are worsening your ADHD symptoms. Once you know which food or drinks are negatively impacting you, you know the things to avoid or cut out completely in the future.

The list usually includes additives, preservatives, sweeteners, and allergenic foods (gluten, dairy, shellfish, wheat, soy, etc.). However, technically you can put anything on the list if you suspect it's worsening or contributing to your symptoms, such as sugar and caffeine.

In this elimination process, you will start with a diet containing none of the items on your list. Your diet will consist of foods that aren't known to worsen symptoms, so any processed foods, sodas, coffee, artificial sweeteners, sugar, and allergenic foods will be eliminated.

After a few days, you start introducing one of the items of food on the list such as sugar for two or three days. If you notice any changes in your behavior, mood, or severity of symptoms after the reintroduction, you are likely sensitive to that item of food. If you don't notice any significant changes, it means that the reintroduced food most likely does not affect your ADHD.

You then move on to the next item on the list until you know exactly how the different foods affect you.

Sensitizing ingredients that should be on your elimination list are as follows:

- preservatives
- butylated hydroxyanisole (BHA)
- sodium benzoate
- butylated hydroxytoluene (BHT)
- sodium nitrate
- tert butylhydroquinone (TBHQ)
- dyes
- FD&C Blue No. 1 and No. 2
- FD&C Yellow No. 5 (tartrazine) and No. 6
- FD&C Green No. 3
- Orange B
- Citrus Red No. 2
- FD&C Red No. 3 and No. 40 (allura)
- foods
- processed and packaged foods
- sugar
- trans fats

- allergenic foods (gluten, dairy, shellfish, wheat, soy, etc.)
- ice cream
- yogurt
- fish high in mercury
- soda
- fruit juice
- fast food
- red meat
- frozen fruits and vegetables (fresh are preferred)

Following a diet that excludes all the above mentioned foods and drinks may be very restrictive, but keep in mind that it only has to be done for a few days at a time. If you are unable to create a meal plan that eliminates all the ingredients mentioned, try cycling through them. It may not be as effective in concluding which specific foods are worsening your symptoms, but you might notice somewhat of a difference when you exclude dairy or red meat for a few days versus when you continually consume it.

Based on this you will be able to get an idea of which foods you should avoid, and which aren't affecting you.

Foods to Consume

Just like some foods may worsen the severity of ADHD symptoms, there are foods on the other end of the spectrum that might actually reduce symptoms. Granted, the list is dramatically shorter than the list of foods that could potentially negatively affect your ADHD, but at the very least, you can be sure that these foods won't make things worse.

Feel free to use this as a guide if you are planning on trying the elimination diet. But be sure to include all necessary food groups into your meals (excluding dairy if you're trying to avoid it).

Omega fatty acids, specifically omega-3, are important for brain function and maintaining optimal brain health. They reduce inflammation in the brain, which is characterized in many mental disorders. They also help form healthy cell membranes, which can improve your brain cells' ability to capture and respond to neurotransmitters (dopamine, serotonin, ephedrine, etc.), leading to improved focus and attentiveness and reduced hyperactivity and impulsivity.

Foods that contain high levels of omega-3 fatty acids include

- salmon, herring, and sardines
- walnuts
- avocados
- seaweed
- chia, hemp, and flax seeds
- flaxseed and canola oil

Protein is the most crucial part of your diet since it is vital for many processes in the body, including the production of neurotransmitters (such as dopamine), which is oftentimes thought to be one of the leading causes of ADHD and EFD.

Foods that are a great source of protein include

- poultry (chicken, turkey, duck)
- seafood
- nuts and seeds
- beans and legumes (chickpeas, black beans, lima beans, kidney beans, lentils)

Foods that are high in antioxidants contain a compound known as polyphenol. These compounds are great for reducing oxidative stress, which is believed to contribute to the symptoms of ADHD (Verlaet et al., 2018).

Oxidative stress is when too many free radicals (a type of unstable molecule that forms during the natural metabolic process in the body) build up in your system. These free radicals can actually harm or damage your other molecules and even your DNA. Antioxidants prevent and protect your cells and the DNA within them from possible damage that can be caused by free radicals.

Foods that have antioxidative properties are

- berries (blackberries, strawberries, blueberries, cranberries, raspberries)
- non-starchy vegetables (spinach, shallots, yellow onions. broccoli, carrots, beetroot, asparagus, bell peppers)
- green tea
- herbs and spices (cloves, garlic, cinnamon, oregano, thyme, ginger, turmeric, rosemary, sage, mint)
- cocoa powder (contains caffeine so it's best to avoid it if you're sensitive to caffeine)

Vitamin B, specifically vitamin B6 and B12, can improve brain function and support brain chemistry, which might be beneficial to people with ADHD and EFD. A deficiency in vitamin B can contribute to mental confusion, fatigue, and forgetfulness, which might worsen the already similar symptoms of ADHD.

Foods that contain high levels of vitamin B6 and B12 are

- pork
- beef liver
- tuna, salmon, and clams
- potatoes and sweet potatoes
- bananas, papayas, and cantaloupes
- mushrooms
- citrus fruits (oranges, lemons, clementines)

- dark leafy greens (spinach, Swiss chard, arugula, kale, collard greens)

Just as a final note: Foods can affect us all in many different ways, whether you have ADHD and EFD or not. The difference is people with ADHD and EFD might be more sensitive to how certain foods affect them, whereas it might not be as severe of a reaction in a neurotypical person. Regardless, knowing what type of foods or ingredients to avoid or restrict, and which ones to add to your diet, can make your life easier. Not only will you feel better and be healthier in general, but there might be a noticeable difference in the severity of your symptoms.

With all that being said, it might be possible that food doesn't affect your ADHD in any noteworthy way at all. Eliminating potentially triggering food does not work for everyone, but it's worth trying it out and seeing if it works for you. Even if it doesn't, remember that mental and physical health go hand in hand, and a healthy, balanced diet is always recommended for improving overall mental health in addition to physical well-being.

Hygiene

Hygiene is an integral part of self-care since it involves taking care of your physical body by bathing or showering, brushing your teeth, washing your hands often, etc. I'm sure you know what hygiene is and why it's important, but it goes deeper than just avoiding potentially dangerous illness-causing bacteria and viruses.

Of course, not falling sick is a huge incentive for hygiene and the most important factor, but it also affects your self-esteem and self-image as well as how others perceive you.

Personal Hygiene

There are many aspects of personal hygiene that need to be taken into consideration, such as toilet hygiene, shower hygiene, nail hygiene, teeth hygiene, sickness hygiene, hand hygiene, and even sleep hygiene.

They're all pretty self-explanatory and include things that you most likely already know like washing your hands after using the toilet and before handling food or eating; showering often; keeping your nails trimmed and clean; brushing your teeth regularly; and preventing spreading germs when you're sick.

Potential consequences of not taking care of personal hygiene range from mild to severe. Not showering or bathing often can cause body odor, greasy hair or skin, and acne or breakouts, which affect your confidence. Not brushing your teeth can lead to cavities and plaque buildup that causes bad breath, pain, and gum disease. Not washing your hands could make you fall ill with a stomach bug or other virus.

Personal Hygiene Routine

With ADHD, mundane tasks like personal hygiene often-times feel more like a chore, but they don't have to. By including strategies in your hygiene routines, you can make it something that you look forward to.

Personal hygiene falls under self-care, meaning it can absolutely be calming and enjoyable. It also doesn't have to be repetitive or boring. You can easily switch it up by alternating between taking a bath one day and a shower the next. Or following an in-depth skincare routine three times a week, and on the days that you don't, you could focus on other things such as trimming body hair or cutting your nails.

Listening to an audiobook, podcast, or music is also a great way to bring more enjoyment to your routine.

Set a reminder and have all the steps to your personal hygiene routine written out and placed somewhere you can easily see it, such as sticking it to the mirror.

An example of a simple nightly hygiene routine is showering or taking a bath, flossing and brushing your teeth, and applying moisturizer. A few times a week, you can add in things like washing your hair, shaving or trimming body or facial hair, clipping your nails, exfoliating, and applying a hair, face, or foot mask.

Sleep Hygiene

Sleep is important for us all; however, many people with ADHD struggle to get a good night's sleep. Whether you have insomnia or wake up frequently during the night for no apparent reason, feeling fatigued from lack of quality sleep will definitely contribute to more severe symptoms.

Lack of sleep creates a snowball effect in people with ADHD. You're already struggling to get through the day and do everything you need to, and sleep deprivation just adds another layer of difficulty. And because you're so tired, stressed, and overwhelmed, you struggle even more to settle down and get a good night's sleep.

So even if you wanted to make an effort to better yourself and take charge of your ADHD symptoms, you're just too tired.

I'm not saying that sleep hygiene is the be-all and end-all of managing ADHD, but it might just help you catch up on some rest so you have the necessary energy and motivation to be able to make other changes in your life that might further improve your ability to function with ADHD.

Sleep hygiene is all about creating healthy sleeping habits. Everything you do during the day right up until you fall asleep contributes to the quality of sleep you're going to get.

So here are some things you could try that might help you sleep better:

- Be consistent.
- Aim for at least seven hours of sleep every night.
- Also, try to go to sleep and wake up at the same time every day. I understand that this might be difficult on weekends or when it's school holidays, but programming your internal sleep cycle to be more predictable will make it easier to wake up and fall asleep.
- If you feel like you need the extra sleep, take a nap during the day.
- Put away the phone.
- At least an hour before you plan to go to sleep, put your phone on charge and on "do not disturb" to avoid any temptations to use it, or leave it in a completely different room in the house if you can't resist checking your social media before bed.
- A good distraction from your phone can be starting your nightly personal hygiene routine during this time.
- Relax.
- Listen to calm, soothing music, meditate, do some light stretching, or reflect on how you're feeling for a few minutes right before bed.

- Avoid doing homework or thinking about stressful things that happened during the day or what might happen tomorrow. Just exist in the moment.
- Limit caffeine.
- If you are drinking coffee, don't have any past noon. Caffeine can stay in your system for up to seven hours after ingesting it. Also, keep in mind that chocolate also contains caffeine so you should avoid chocolate during this time as well.
- Improve your sleep environment.
- Adjust your room to suit all your sleeping preferences. Make sure you have a comfortable pillow and mattress and wash your sheets and linens often (at least once every two weeks).
- If you wake up easily because of external noises, get some earplugs or soundproof your walls. If you hate the quiet, invest in a white noise machine or a radio. If you prefer a cooler temperature, get a desk fan. If you're sensitive to light, change your curtains to dark or blackout ones.
- Use your bed for sleep only.
- When you work, read, scroll Instagram, or do homework from your bed, your mind will have a hard time associating the bed with sleep. Instead, place a comfortable chair in the corner of your room for scrolling the internet during the day, do your homework at your desk or the dining room table, etc.

- Sleep is for the tired.
- This may sound counterintuitive, but try not to get in bed until you're feeling tired. If you do feel tired and you don't fall asleep within 20 minutes, get up, take a bathroom break, drink some water or tea, or just do something that's calming until you feel tired again.
- When you're struggling to fall asleep, tossing and turning will just lead to frustration, making it even more difficult to fall asleep.
- Limit your naps.
- If you feel like you need a nap, try to take one earlier in the day and limit it to 30–45 minutes.
- Journal.
- Writing down your thoughts, feelings, and the events of the day that made you feel stressed or overwhelmed is a good way to get them out of your mind, so you don't think about them when you're trying to fall asleep.
- If you're afraid you might forget something important, write out your to-do list for the next day or the next few days and then try to stay present in a calm state of mind.

5

PRODUCTIVITY

Being productive in life means adopting a mindset of continuous improvement, meaning everything you do is pushing you a fraction closer to your ultimate goals. This, however, doesn't mean you shouldn't take time for yourself or do things that bring you joy even if it doesn't directly benefit you in the long run.

What I mean by this is that spending time on yourself (even if you're just doing nothing) might not seem like it's productive, but it is important to avoid burnout in the future. Of course, if you spend the majority of your time doing nothing, that's not going to get you to where you want to be in life in any aspect.

The trick is to create a balance where you're still doing your best to be productive but not overexert yourself. And since people with ADHD tend to lean towards either end of the extreme (either doing nothing or doing everything), it's especially important to create a healthy balance.

Time Management

People with ADHD and EFD aren't motivated by future deadlines or possible consequences as much as neurotypical people are. And the further away the deadline or consequence is, the less pressure they feel to complete the task. When the due date for a project is less than a day away, the pressure becomes too much to ignore any longer and that pressure is what motivates them to actually start.

The overarching issue with time management for people with ADHD or EFD is they overestimate the amount of time they have left or underestimate how long something will take them to do. They also have a hard time keeping track of what is due when, or they lose track of time and spend way too much time on one task, throwing off their entire schedule for the day.

A possible solution to this is having a big analog clock in your direct line of sight when sitting at your desk. It might take some effort to get into the habit of checking it every once in a while, but it might help you stay on track with your to-do list and prevent you from spending hours on a task that you only planned to spend half an hour on. However, setting an alarm clock might be just as efficient.

Another strategy that could help motivate you to do something earlier rather than later is visualizing future emotions. By reminding yourself of past experiences where you had to pull an all-nighter to finish a project, you could use that to motivate yourself to start earlier. Using the unpleasant memories and emotions of the past, you can then tell yourself how much less pressure and stress it would cause to break up a project into several sessions or parts and have it completed a day before it's due instead of trying to do the whole thing the night before. Ask yourself how good it will feel to not have to worry about it and how proud you will be of yourself handing in a project that's not rushed.

Time management is all about prioritizing future goals over present desires. Playing the new video game your parents got you is much more enticing than doing research for a project that's only due in a week. But that's exactly the situation where you should practice restraint and keep future goals in mind in the present. In this scenario, you could use the game as a reward. Set aside an hour to do research or plan for the assignment, once the timer goes off, you're free to play your game. Not only will you get the satisfaction of playing video games, but you will also feel less guilty and more confident in yourself for putting off your immediate desire for future gain.

Here are some ways that might make you more mindful of time:

- Plan your priorities in advance.
- Whether you plan ahead for the entire week or day by day, write down what needs to be done and when you plan on starting them as well as completing them. Make sure to block out enough time to ensure you don't run out of time and set reminders.
- Find external accountability.
- Tell a parent when you're planning on starting a task and have them check in on you to help hold you accountable and to avoid procrastination.
- Set multiple deadlines.
- When you receive an assignment, break it into several smaller tasks and have deadlines for each of them. For example, you have to write a speech that's due in two weeks. You could break it down into research, planning, first draft, editing, final draft, and memorizing. Research should be done by Tuesday, planning done by Thursday, first draft by Monday, editing and final draft by Wednesday, and use Thursday for memorizing. Having multiple deadlines puts more pressure on you which might help motivate you to get started.
- Reward yourself.
- Give yourself an incentive for sticking to your schedule or getting everything done on your to-do list for the day. Try not to reward yourself with food since this might create an unhealthy relationship

with it, leading to eating disorders and potential health problems.

- Finish before your bedtime routine starts.
- Have a set time every night for when you should start with your bedtime routine and aim to finish all schoolwork before then. This will, again, put some pressure on you to finish your tasks earlier rather than later.

Eat The Frog First

Speaking of doing things earlier rather than later, the term "eat the frog first" is from a quote from Mark Twain, and it's a popular phrase that helps a lot of people prioritize effectively and stay productive.

The principle of this saying is that if you have to eat a frog every day, do it first thing in the morning so that you don't have to worry about it for the rest of the day (Childs, 2007). Your frog could be anything: homework, cleaning your room, folding laundry, or doing the dishes.

Every task on your to-do list falls into one of the following categories:

1. Things you don't want to do and don't have to do.
2. Things you don't want to do but have to do.
3. Things you want to do and also have to do.

4. Things you want to do but don't have to do.

The things you don't want to do but have to do are the frogs, and these should be at the top of your to-do list since they're, by comparison, the most dreaded tasks. Instead of putting it off until the last minute when you're tired and have even less motivation to do it, you should get it done as soon as possible.

Since people with ADHD and EFD usually have a hard time prioritizing their daily tasks and activities, using this method can help them reach their long-term goals by working on them a little bit every day.

The process is simple: Identify your frog (the task you don't want to do but need to do every day) and eat it (do it) as soon as possible. With school taking up the majority of your day, doing something that takes time first thing in the morning can be unrealistic.

Here are some more tips that could help you gain momentum and stay productive:

- Don't put it down, put it away.
- The biggest reason for a messy room or an unorganized desk is using an item and just putting it down when you're done, fully intent on putting it away later. But then three weeks pass and it's still in

the same spot and you just can't get yourself to put it back in its designated place.

- This goes for virtually anything: laundry, dishes, the stapler, art supplies, or anything else that you pick up or use. This is also why it's important to have a place for everything, so you don't end up with a desk so cluttered it's unusable.
- Be productive in procrastination.
- This might not work for people who are not good at multitasking. But if you are the type of person to get bored doing one task from start to finish, you can try procrastinating on one specific task by starting on another. For example, if you get bored of doing homework halfway through, start cleaning and organizing your backpack before continuing homework.
- Again, this may not work for everyone since it's very easy to end up with eight unfinished tasks without having the energy or motivation to go back and finish any of them.
- Try juggling two or three tasks at first just to test whether this strategy might work for you.
- Use the Pomodoro technique.
- This method encourages you to get more done in less time. It's essentially a timer system where you break down all the things you have to get done in a day into 25-minute sprints followed by 5minute

breaks. Once you've done 2 or 3 rounds of sprints, you can take a longer break (20-30 minutes).

- There are plenty of Pomodoro timing apps that also have built-in virtual reward systems for every completed sprint. Or you could just use your phone to set a timer and only work on a single task for 25 minutes, take a 5-minute break, and continue with the same task for another 25 minutes or start another task completely and work on that for 25 minutes.

- It's important that you not get overly distracted during your 5-minute breaks so avoid going on social media during this time. The idea is to try to get as much done in 25 minutes as possible. Even if you don't finish the task, you still made progress and you could always continue with the same task after the 5-minute break.

- Beat procrastination with the 5-minute rule.

- This is a cognitive behavioral technique that focuses on beating procrastination by just getting you started with a task you tend to put off. Usually, the hardest part of getting something done is the initial act of starting.

- Set a 5-minute timer and then start on whatever it is you need to get done. After the timer goes off, you have the choice of either stopping or continuing. What tends to happen is after the five-minute mark, the hardest part is over and continuing doesn't feel as intimidating or overwhelming anymore.

- This technique is great for building the necessary momentum to be able to follow through, simply commit five minutes to the most difficult task on your to-do list, and more often than not, you will end up completing the task because it's likely not as difficult as you thought it would be.
- Turn it into a game.
- I've mentioned looking at mundane activities as side quests in a video game, but you could also turn it into an adrenaline-filled rush by trying to complete a task as quickly as possible or even setting a timer and trying to get it done before it hits zero.
- Telling yourself "I bet I can clean my room in less than 15 minutes" turns into a high-stakes race to prove to yourself that you actually can do it. And even if you don't succeed, your room will still be cleaner at the end of the 15 minutes than it was before, and you've got your heart racing and some physical movement as a bonus. It's a win-win.
- Be kind to yourself.
- Remember that when you struggle to focus or start on a task that you really need to get done, it's not because you're lazy or a failure. You have a neurological condition that affects your brain's capacity to focus and remain on task.

- It's not your fault and reverting to shaming yourself
  or telling yourself you're worthless will not do
  anything except make you hate yourself. You won't
  blame the sky for bad weather, so why blame
  yourself for something that's not in your control?

Your best is always good enough. Don't attribute your productivity to your self-worth. Regardless of how much or how little you get done on any given day, be proud of yourself for navigating through a world where the majority of people don't have to deal with what you need to deal with every single day.

Problem-Solving

Problem-solving relies heavily on decision-making, which can be overwhelming for teenagers who have ADHD or EFD. When an obstacle pops up in your life, big or small, being able to overcome it is essential for present benefit and future reference. But when you have ADHD or EFD, the process of solving a problem or even identifying potential problems can be hard. Because there's so much uncertainty over what to do and what's the right way to solve it, they shut down. This often results in no resolutions, so the problem stays a persistent issue.

Impulsivity can further derail any positive outcome since your first reaction to conflict is often driven by emotion, and you might end up saying or doing something that escalates the situation, making it even harder to diffuse later on.

The process of solving a problem or overcoming an obstacle involves several steps: identifying the problem or obstacle, thinking of possible solutions, a breakdown of the preferred solution, implementing the solution, assessing the results, and mediating.

We will be going through each of these stages and explaining in as much detail how you can implement them in everyday scenarios. As with most mental skills, problem-solving is one that can be improved through practice and patience.

Identify the Problem

Before you can solve a problem, you need to be aware of it. But knowing that there's a problem won't help you solve it unless you can identify what is the root of the issue or what is causing it to be ongoing.

Let's use a simple example for this. The overarching problem is you tend to be late for school. Now you need to ask questions about the problem to be able to get down to the core of the issue. Why is this a problem? Because you miss out on class, or you get in trouble. Or maybe being late is stressful and makes you feel unproductive. Another important question you can ask is what is causing you to be late. Are you snoozing the alarm until you only have 10 minutes before you have to leave for school? Maybe your morning routine is chaotic, and you have way too much to do in a small amount of time.

Whatever the reasons may be, being aware of the specifics is crucial to solving the problem.

Possible Solutions

Once you know the reasons why the problem exists, you can start brainstorming solutions. Write down all the reasons for the problem and as many resolutions as possible for each one.

Don't worry about prioritization or order, just let the words flow and come up with as many solutions as you can think of without judgment.

Using our previous example, possible solutions for snoozing the alarm too many times could be going to bed earlier if you still wake up feeling tired in the morning; setting multiple alarms to go off in one-minute intervals (the idea is to bombard you with alarms every minute so you don't have enough time between each one to fall asleep again); leaving your phone across the room so you have to get out of bed to snooze the alarm; or sitting up and drinking some water as soon as the first alarm goes off.

For a chaotic morning routine, some solutions include completing some of it the night before such as packing your school bag, picking out an outfit, and preparing lunch.

Simplify your morning routine by cutting out some less important tasks or chores, such as making your bed. Taking a shower in the evenings instead of in the mornings can also help reduce the time you spend getting ready for school.

Break It Down

The list of possible solutions won't be perfect, and the possibility of facing even more obstacles by implementing the solutions to try and fix the original problem might be overwhelming. So to try and avoid that, you can break down your list of solutions even further to make it more manageable.

All this means is you want to go into even more detail with regard to resolving your problem.

Again, using the example before, you can investigate why you still feel tired in the mornings when your alarm goes off. If you're getting less than eight hours of sleep, that's likely to be the problem. If you are getting enough sleep and still wake up tired, it might be worth talking to your primary healthcare practitioner to rule out any possible health-related issues, such as low iron levels or sleep apnea.

Regardless, in this step, you also want to break down your list of solutions into steps you can take to implement them. Step one: Visit the doctor to rule out concerns over morning fatigue. Step 2: Reduce screen time before bed. Step 3: Minimize morning routine. Step 4: Pack school bag, choose an outfit, and shower the night before.

Implement a Solution

Pick the solution you feel most confident in and have a trial period where you implement it for a few days. This will allow you to see firsthand whether it's solving the problem or not. Don't give up on it if it's not fixing the issue straight away.

If you come across potential pitfalls or unforeseen problems with the solution you picked, tweak a few things and try again. Also, don't be afraid to ask for input from others such as a supportive and understanding parent or friend. Sometimes a third-party can help you see the bigger picture since you may have some blindspots when you're in the middle of everything.

When the solution you tried is not working despite your best efforts, move on to the next potential one.

Assessing Progress

Remember, we're not looking for perfection. If you're seeing positive results, it usually means you're on the right path. Give yourself credit where it's due. If you were always half an hour late, and after implementing some resolutions you're only 15 minutes late, that's still an accomplishment to be proud of.

From here, you can then continue to change some things or try different approaches and see if it's making the problem better or worse. Every step in the right direction will lead you closer to overcoming the problem.

Mediating

Asking for help is always an option. Resolving the problems that are affecting us negatively is hard, even for people who don't have ADHD or EFD. Admitting that you need help is better than being stuck in a situation you can't seem to escape.

If you have friends or family members that you trust to give you the right advice, go to them for it. Alternatively, counselors, therapists, and ADHD coaches can offer some practical solutions and strategies that can help you improve your problem-solving abilities.

The best help is the kind that will eventually not be needed anymore. You don't need people to spoon-feed you and look over your shoulder every second of the day. Instead, you need guidance, support, and knowledge to be able to overcome future obstacles on your own.

Cognitive Flexibility

Nothing in life is stagnant. Changes happen all the time— some are small, and some are life-changing. Cognitive flexibility is your mind's ability to accept and adapt to new, changing, or unplanned circumstances and situations and to regulate your reactions to them.

If you are someone who dislikes or feels uncomfortable with change to the point where you avoid it at all costs, you might benefit from improving your cognitive flexibility. Some signs of poor cognitive flexibility are: thinking in black-and-white terms (something is either right or wrong, good or bad, etc. There's no neutral ground or "gray area"), perfectionism, fear of the unknown, need for control, fixed mindset (unable to change perspectives), and avoidance of confrontation or debate.

Cognitive flexibility is important for learning, solving problems creatively, and responding well to the ever-changing environments we are exposed to in an efficient manner.

The best way to improve cognitive flexibility is by exposing yourself to new situations. However, this can be very triggering and overwhelming to people with ADHD and EFD so a better way to approach it would be to do so slowly and cautiously. So here are some easy and practical things you can do that will help improve your cognitive flexibility:

- Alter your daily schedule.
- This will obviously not apply to everything, but there are likely some things on your everyday to-do

list that don't have to happen in a specific order. Things like making your bed, taking a short walk (and taking a different route each time), working on a skill or hobby, and doing homework are all things that are time-flexible, meaning you can do them at any point during the day unless you're in school that is.

- Play around with your tasks and responsibilities and mix them up. Not only will this avoid getting bored with your routine, but it also improves your cognitive flexibility.

- Alternatively, you could also change how you do certain things. If you always wash your body in a certain order or fold your clothes a certain way, try doing it differently. This will also help you figure out the most sensible and efficient way to do things.

- Look for opportunities to experience something new.

- This does not include things that are dangerous and harmful. Take on a new hobby or learn a new skill, try different foods, explore your town or city, make a new friend, volunteer at the pet shelter, or watch that movie you've been putting off for years.

- With every experience, you learn something new, and as a bonus, it can also encourage the release of dopamine in the brain, which we know is great for motivation, learning, and memory.

- Try creative thinking.
- Instead of trying to think within the confines of what is real and practical, think outside that box and come up with creative and unusual ways to solve problems.
- This is also known as divergent thinking, and it involves thinking in a manner that is unlimited to what is possible and what isn't. The goal is not to solve problems this way, but rather to encourage creative reasoning and become more open or aware of different perspectives.
- Take the narrow path.
- Modern technology has undoubtedly made our lives easier, but that's not necessarily a good thing when it comes to cognitive flexibility. Our phones have become a crutch for solving problems, from spellcheck to depending on the calculator for the simplest of equations. We're not giving our minds the opportunity to overcome even the smallest of obstacles, so when it comes to solving more complex problems, we're completely lost.
- Seek out different opinions.
- When you surround yourself with people who only share your exact views, opinions, and beliefs, you create an echo chamber of confirmation bias that solidifies your thought processes. Since everyone in

your circle agrees with you, you have no reason to question your perspective or reasoning.

- By communicating with people who have diverse opinions, views, beliefs, and perspectives, your mind opens up to the idea that there's more than one way of viewing the world around you and that someone else's reasoning can still be morally correct.
- Even if you don't agree with someone else's opinion or belief, the ability to understand where they're coming from and why they might see things the way they do is an aspect of cognitive flexibility.
- It might be hard at first to not want to distance yourself from people who have an opposing perspective, but conversations between people who have a different opinion are vital in a world where nothing is as straightforward as we think and where two things can be true at once. Friendly debates are food for thought, for all parties involved, and agreeing to disagree doesn't have to mean the end of a friendship.

6

SOCIAL LIFE AND SCHOOL

Having a healthy social life while also prioritizing school can be difficult, especially considering all the changes and extra responsibilities that come with growing up. Social media is a great tool to enhance your real-life relationships, but it can also negatively impact your self-esteem and ability to connect with your peers in a way that's meaningful and fulfilling.

ADHD can affect your social life because of many different reasons. You might have a hard time picking up on social cues, get bored with a conversation and stop listening (which may offend others), interrupt often (so you come off as rude), or say something without thinking. Or you may forget to reply to messages or keep in touch over the summer holidays, leading them to think you don't have any interest in continuing the friendship.

The best way to build lasting friendships is to be open about your ADHD or EFD and make them aware of the symptoms and repercussions from the start. A genuine, kind person won't judge or bully you for it but rather be understanding and try to help where they can.

Another good way to ensure your friendships last is by making friends that share your interests. Starting a friendship with someone who's in your art class or on the same team during extracurricular activities will ensure you see them often without having to remember to reply to a text from them.

In this chapter, we will discuss how social media impacts you and how to break free of the unnecessary pressure it puts on you as well as how to have a social life if you're still a student.

Social Media

The biggest problem with social media is the amount of time you spend on it without even realizing it. If you go into your phone's settings and look for your screen time statistics, you might be surprised to find that that number is much higher than you thought.

· · ·

The Effects of Social Media on ADHD

Social media is designed to keep your attention and hook you on the dopamine that's released every time someone likes your photo, or you see a funny or relatable meme. They want you to spend hours scrolling an endless supply of content because of advertising and marketing reasons. More users mean more sales opportunities.

And even though this is the case with everyone, people who have ADHD or EFD are less prone to being aware of how many hours are wasted looking at a screen. When you reach for your phone to quickly look at the time, you see a notification. The urge to check it is your brain asking for a dopamine "hit" because social media is addictive.

The dopamine that's released by completing something on your to-do list is way less and requires more effort than just opening up an app. Every time you see someone engaged with your post or you watch a funny video, the reward system in your brain is activated. That's why it's also much easier for people with ADHD and EFD to get hooked on social media

So, you're spending hours a day on social media, and you feel good while the screen is in front of your face. But what happens after is you feel guilty, ashamed, and useless because you haven't done a single thing and it's already past six in the afternoon. And it doesn't help that everyone online seems to have their life together, which is not even true.

When you're comparing your behind-the-scenes with someone else's highlight reels, your brain starts believing that you're not good enough and never will be. It can also lead to unrealistic expectations of your progress or what you are able to handle when implementing lifestyle changes.

Another factor that comes into play is how social media can worsen symptoms of ADHD and EFD. Since bad news gets more engagement, the algorithms are more likely to push stories and articles containing topics of shock value that may leave you feeling anxious, worried, or even depressed. This unnecessary stress is carried with you even after you exit the app.

In fact, one study shows that not only will social media worsen your symptoms of ADHD, but it could also potentially lead to developing ADHD symptoms even if you don't have it (Ra et al., 2018).

If you find yourself constantly distracted by your phone, the computer, or even video games for more than two or three hours a day, you might benefit from cutting down on some of your screen time.

A person with ADHD may experience boredom more intensely than the average neurotypical individual, and reaching for the phone is a quick and easy way to resolve this issue. But at what cost? Chances are you're going to have a hard time putting it down, and in the process, you'll neglect other tasks and responsibilities, leaving you feeling worse mentally.

The more you use social media, the more you'll want to use it. That's just how addiction works. Your brain builds a tolerance to the amount of dopamine being released when you scroll social media, so eventually it won't be satisfied with the same amount and you'll need to scroll for longer and longer to get the same effect as before. And that's how you end up spending nine hours a day on apps and still somehow feel like you need more.

Breaking the Cycle

So how can you break the cycle with your sanity intact? And what is the best way to do it? Would it be better to go cold turkey or wean yourself off it slowly but surely?

When dealing with something as complex and difficult as ADHD or EFD where you might not be able to control your impulses or limit the amount of time you spend on social media, a sudden withdrawal might be your best option.

I know it sounds daunting, but I promise you'll get through it. And with time you'll realize that you feel better emotionally without it and won't even miss it anymore. However, going cold turkey can be reserved as a last resort if you're struggling with other strategies to limit social media use.

Chances are your phone has a built-in system that lets you limit screen time and access to certain apps. Though, the problem with this is that you can simply disable the feature at any time and continue scrolling. You would really need dedication and resilience to abide by the time limits you set up.

Here are a few alternative methods you can try to implement to limit the time you spend on social media:

- Download an accountability app.
- There are apps available that incentivize you with digital rewards for not using your phone. Again, the main issue with this is you can decide to disable or ignore it fairly easily and quickly at any time.
- Use self-talk.
- Remind yourself that you can't afford to waste any more time on social media, so you shouldn't even go on it to begin with because your brain won't allow you to do anything else once you're on your phone.
- Hide social media apps.
- Hiding the apps you tend to lose hours on in a folder somewhere where you have to navigate multiple menus on your home screen can prevent you from seeing them and getting tempted to use them when you're just opening up your phone to use the calculator, for example. Also, knowing that it will take a little more effort to get to them as opposed to

being easily accessible from the home screen can make a difference.

- Disable or uninstall social media apps temporarily.
- Committing to a social media fast for a few days might make you realize that living without it isn't as bad as you thought. You might be a little bored, but it might make it easier to get some things done that have been on your to-do list for weeks or months.
- Many teens with ADHD say that deep cleaning their room and even shuffling around the furniture into a new layout gives them a substantial amount of dopamine and satisfaction.
- Use social media as a reward.
- Make a rule that if you complete all (or even just most) of the things you wanted to do on any given day, you're allowed to use your phone for an hour or two. Though, this still has the potential of turning into a six-hour binge, and all of a sudden it's almost midnight and you're still on your phone.
- Limit the number of social media apps you use.
- Instead of having a plethora of apps to switch between when you get bored of one, stick to keeping only one or two and get rid of the rest. You'll likely end up getting bored of both of them at some point and put down the phone instead of opening up a new one that has a different user interface and type

of content that might keep you entertained for
another two hours.

The hardest part of this process is sticking with your inten-
tions to follow through with your strategy. If you're unable to
restrict your social media usage, stopping it completely might
be the only way to sever the attachment you have with it.

While social media can be a useful tool to keep in touch with
long-distance friends and family members, try to keep socializing through calls and texts as opposed to social media apps.
Make friends that live close by, like down the street or in the
same suburb, to limit the need for interaction via social
media.

School

The secret to staying on top of schoolwork is an effective organizational system that's not complicated or requires more
than one or two steps to uphold or manage. If the system
requires a lot of upkeep and effort, you'll most likely not stick
with it.

Some strategies will definitely require some adjustments, so
they fit in with your schedule or routine as well as your preferences. A few techniques you can try out to help you
manage and organize your schoolwork as easy as possible so

you still have time to have a social life and partake in other hobbies include

- Get clear binders or files for every individual subject.
- These help you to avoid losing homework or assignments. However, don't get a designated homework folder since it can still accumulate junk and unnecessary paperwork. Instead, put the homework for a class in that subject's designated file or folder and check all of them when you do homework.
- Avoid classroom stimuli.
- Ask the teacher to seat you away from windows, doors, and other distractions. It may also help to be as close to the front as possible to limit distractions from your classmates.
- Take pictures.
- If you did not manage to finish copying slides or writing down information from the board, ask the teacher if you could take pictures of it so you can finish it later when you're doing homework.
- Use a fidget toy.
- Ask the teacher if you may be allowed to make use of a fidget toy (discreetly and without distracting other students, of course) to counteract hyperactivity.

- Make it up.
- Use silly acronyms, songs, or mnemonics to remember formulas, order of operation, etc. It doesn't have to make sense as long as it helps you remember. If it works, it's not stupid!
- Make use of lists and checklists.
- Use lists and checklists to help you remember what you need to do or what homework you have for the day. Use your phone or a scrap piece of paper you keep in your pocket that you'll see later when you get home. Normally, I wouldn't advocate for writing on yourself, but if you can get a non-toxic pen, write all the subjects you have homework for on the back of your hand. This will prevent you from losing the piece of paper or not checking your notes app and forgetting what homework you have.
- Organize as you go.
- Throw out unimportant paperwork or trash and try to stay organized as much as you can. Throw out trash and sort out clutter that piles up in your locker or bedroom every day which makes it hard to see textbooks and other important items.
- Limit the amount of stationery.
- The more things you have, the more time you'll have to spend organizing everything. Try to keep stationery and clutter to a minimum. Avoid extra items such as colored pens and pencils, highlighters

(except maybe one or two if you study better with them), and other unnecessary trinkets that just take up space. This also goes for your room and desk space. A clean, well-organized space minimizes distractions and keeps everything that is important unobstructed and in sight.

- Have a set time to do homework and work on projects.
- Again, the time that you feel most able to do so will vary, but try to budget at least an hour or two every day to focus on completing school work.
- Don't take off your shoes.
- This might not work for you but a lot of people with ADHD and EFD agree that they're less productive when they take off their shoes. It may be because the brain associates taking off your shoes with being done with work for the day. So if you do want to get dressed in something more comfortable when you get home, put your shoes back on.
- Take care of yourself.
- This was mentioned previously, but I want to stress how important it is to eat well, stay active, and get quality sleep. Chances are you're likely not drinking enough water or getting enough sleep, so try to prioritize these things because it can make a big difference in your energy levels and brain function.

Entertainment

If you don't already have a hobby or area of interest, you probably have one that you've just not discovered yet. Hobbies are not just for entertainment purposes—although they usually involve having fun—they're also essential for mental well-being since they decrease stress, elevate mood and energy levels, and provide you with a sense of fulfillment and satisfaction.

It also gives us the opportunity to learn new skills while expressing ourselves in a healthy and meaningful way. Hobbies provide us with feel-good hormone production in the brain, which is great for ADHD and EFD.

Hobbies

A hobby is defined as anything you do in your free time that brings you happiness. Though, by that definition, scrolling social media or drinking alcohol could also be considered a hobby. However, I like to define a hobby as something you do in your free time that's not only entertaining but also positively contributes to your mental or physical health in both the present and future tense.

For me, a hobby needs to be entertaining, stimulating, and beneficial to some degree. Luckily, there are so many options to choose from that it's virtually impossible not to feel drawn to or interested in one of them.

Just to give you an idea, here's a comprehensive list of hobbies that you can try. Most of them are cost-efficient (meaning you need little to no money to get started) and might even help you develop skills that could be beneficial to a career path.

Nature

Whether you're doing general yard work or creating a garden with beautiful flowers or crisp fruit and vegetables, gardening is a great way to connect with nature and reap the physical and mental benefits of it. You could also choose to just focus on identifying and researching different plants or get into foraging.

Other niches include collecting insects, birdwatching, foraging, hiking, environmental advocacy, and even researching animals. When it comes to the great outdoors, the possibilities are quite literally limitless.

Space

Did you know humans have only explored about 4% of the universe? And since space is constantly expanding, it might even be less. If you're not into the scientific aspect of the universe, there are many other things relating to space that require nothing more than a sincere fascination with it. Astronomy, astrology, tracking constellations, or just stargazing to name a few.

Whether your interest in the sky is serious or casual, thinking about how the possibility of alien life is much more probable than anyone might realize or how we exist floating on a speck in an endless void is sure to strike up an interesting conversation.

Martial Arts

Not only are martial arts a great source of exercise, but they also teach discipline and self-control while strengthening neurological pathways in the brain. Total mind and body coordination help with impulsivity, and the exercise will also help manage hyperactivity.

Drama

While acting is an impressive skill, there are many other routes you can take that all involve a multitude of skill sets, from designing and building sets to writing and producing an amazing play.

Some more hobbies with regard to this are improv, stand-up comedy, makeup (and special effects makeup), lighting and sound design, post-production editing, and even directing.

Language

Learning a language is quicker and easier when you're young. There are plenty of benefits to this. You'll be able to talk to people from a completely different part of the world, and it's something you could add to your resume.

You could also extend this into learning about cultures from all over the world.

Writing

Writing is an effective way to process emotions and decrease mind clutter and overthinking. You can express yourself creatively through storytelling, poetry, journaling, or lyrics.

There's no wrong way to do this, and it will inadvertently improve your grammar, spelling, and vocabulary. You can also use any medium such as your phone's notes app, a laptop, or keep it classic with pen and paper.

Visual Art

Similar to writing, expressing yourself using visual art can be very impactful. This also includes an array of sub-categories such as drawing, painting, digital art, sculpting, pottery, comic book illustration, etc.

Finding your personal style is a journey on its own and can be very fulfilling when other people are amazed by the concepts and visuals you create from your imagination.

Cooking

You're going to have to feed yourself for the rest of your life anyway, so why not make it something that you're good at? Don't just stop at being able to make a banging mac and cheese, challenge yourself to master all the different cuisines from the various countries that the world has to offer.

You'll never have to wonder what you should have for dinner because you'll never run out of ideas. Alternatively, you can create your own recipes and dishes inspired by your own taste and preferences. I think we can all agree that having a delicious meal is not something anyone ever regrets.

Crafting and Thrifting

Creating something beautiful from random unused items is not only stimulating but also requires a lot of creativity. It can also improve your problem-solving abilities due to the nature of crafting requiring the ability to think practically and innovatively.

Turning an old, dilapidated dresser or desk into something that's aesthetically pleasing and suits your style is both rewarding and can be turned into a lucrative side hustle.

It's also way more environmentally friendly than just buying something new from IKEA when something breaks. There's also a plethora of furniture you can make out of pallet wood from desks and side tables to bookshelves and organizational storage.

Music

From playing an instrument and composing a beautiful tune to being able to sing perfect harmonies and develop your vocal range, music is another form of expressive art that requires a lot of attention to detail and passion.

Try your hand at the ukulele—they're fairly inexpensive and are known for being the easiest instrument to master. Many free apps that allow you to compose music on your phone or computer.

If you're not able to join a music class, there are plenty of tutorials on YouTube that will have you jamming on an instrument in no time.

Team Sports

A great way to work on your social skills, discipline, and teamwork is taking on a sport such as football, soccer, volleyball, basketball, baseball, or any other sport you might be interested in that involves teammates working together to achieve a mutual goal.

There are also team-driven activities that don't include running after a ball such as chess, fishing, mathletes, or joining a band or choir.

Mid-Book Review Page

You Can Be Part of a System That Will Help Someone Just Like You

"I haven't failed. I've just found 10,000 ways that won't work." — Thomas Edison

Remember in Chapter 3 when we looked at habits and organization? We talked about how it can be difficult to decide which is the most important or relevant thing out of the list of things that need to happen, and how good organization can help you keep track of everything. Well, sometimes you don't even need to create your own system – sometimes there's already one in place for you to rely on.

Think about cooking a simple meal. If you have all the ingredients laid out in front of you and some memory of what that meal should be like when it's done, you have a fairly good chance of creating it. But if you have a recipe, with clear steps telling you what order things should be done in, you're even more likely to be successful – and you're going to get far less stressed out in the process.

Now imagine choosing that recipe book in the first place. Out of all the books there are to choose from, how do you know that this is the one that's going to give you the guidance you need? Simple! You look at the other system already in place –

the one that's going to guide you to make the right decision – you look at the reviews.

This is your chance to help someone like you find the guidance they need.

By leaving a review of this book on Amazon, you can help other people navigating life with ADHD find the tools that will help them cope.

When you leave your honest opinion of this book and how it's helped you on Amazon, other readers will be able to tell whether it's the right book for them or not – and you will have helped provide that system for someone who really needs it.

Thank you for helping to be part of a structure that will help other people like you find the guidance they're looking for. This is a team effort, and I couldn't do it without you.

"Leave a review of this book on Amazon"

7

TASK INITIATION, COMPLETION, AND PRIORITIZATION

E veryone sometimes puts off activities that are boring, tedious, or time-consuming. Procrastination is a human trait. However, it becomes worrisome when it negatively affects your life such as causing you to get bad grades.

Several executive functioning skills come into play when getting started on a task and following through until it's completed besides just task initiation. Though, task initiation is usually the biggest contributor to procrastination.

This chapter will focus on what you can do, realistically, to overcome procrastination and complete a task from start to finish as well as some basic prioritization strategies.

Task Initiation

Task initiation is simply the act of starting a task or activity. For someone with ADHD or EFD, it can be difficult to do even when every fiber of your being is yelling at you to just get started.

Completing tasks and responsibilities that you have no interest in or motivation to do can be mental torture if you have ADHD or EFD. Getting started with a task requires the most amount of energy and motivation—something that a person with ADHD or EFD has very little of on a good day.

That's why working on just getting the ball rolling should be the main priority. Think of task initiation as pushing a boulder off a cliff. The most amount of energy will be needed when you initially push it, but once it's over the edge, the momentum takes over and the hardest part is done with. The problem is gathering the energy to push the boulder in the first place.

Task initiation requires energy and motivation from everyone, but for people with ADHD and EFD, the boulder feels much heavier and, therefore, is harder to push. Also, usually their internal motivation isn't enough. Instead, they depend on external motivation, such as pressure, stress, and consequences to be able to start a task.

Even tasks that might be enjoyable for people with ADHD or EFD can become impossible to start because of poor task initiation. Procrastination can even occur with things such as hobbies or playing video games that seem like too much effort to begin with.

When you have a deadline, such as a school project due date, the sense of urgency is usually what gets a person with ADHD or EFD to start. However, if there's no deadline or harsh consequences (like when you need to clean your room), your mind will turn to emotions like guilt and shame to get you moving. This is obviously not ideal and can have very negative effects on your mental health.

Here are some healthier ways to overcome procrastination:

- Build momentum and use it to your advantage.
- Start on a simple, small task that isn't as intimidating, such as placing your lunchbox in the dishwasher when you get home from school. From there you can move on to removing all the books for the subjects you have homework for and placing them on your desk. Then go through your school bag and remove all clutter or loose paperwork, sort through them, and discard the unimportant papers or trash.

- By utilizing the momentum from a smaller, easier task, you may get more done as long as you don't stay stagnant for too long. If you feel you do need a break, just sit down (without any distractions such as your phone) for a few minutes before continuing.
- Reduce the task size.
- Thinking about how much energy you would need to complete a project or assignment for school or how long it will take to clean your room can be demotivating and overwhelming. Instead of thinking about the task in its entirety from start to finish, decide what's the first step and focus only on doing that.
- For example, if your room is extremely messy because you haven't had the time or energy to clean it in two months, don't group all the steps that you'll need to follow to clean it. That's way too general and vague. Start with one goal such as taking all the dirty dishes and empty water bottles to the kitchen or picking up all the trash. Once you've done that, you've already gotten past the hardest part (getting started) and the room will already look better and more manageable, plus you've completed the task you set out to do. You are then free to move on to the next step.
- Gain confidence and practice.

- By completing smaller tasks (as described in the previous bullet point), you'll gain more confidence in your ability to initiate tasks. The more you prove to yourself that you are capable of getting stuff done, the easier it will be to overcome that initial block because you believe in yourself.
- Use the if/then strategy.
- This is very similar to a reward system and works by providing you with an incentive to start on a task. Examples of this can be "if I finish my homework early, then I can play video games or browse social media for a few hours before bedtime without feeling guilty about it" or "if I finish this part of my project today, then I'll have less to do at a later date." It's not a perfect system, but the goal is to get you to start somewhere.
- Get rid of fear.
- Many times, people with ADHD will procrastinate on a certain task because they're afraid they're not smart or good enough to do something, or they fear they might fail, or the end result won't be perfect. Once you get rid of the idea that something has to be done perfectly or not at all, you'll appreciate the process much more.

I FEEL like people with ADHD sometimes forget that to do something well, you first have to do it badly. There's no such thing as natural talent, just perseverance. As long as you're willing and determined to work on your executive functioning skills, they will improve over time.

Focus and Task Completion

A lack of focus is easily the most recognizable symptom of ADHD and EFD since it's the symptom that affects a person's ability to thrive the most. It interferes with everyday activities and impacts almost every aspect of your life. You need to be able to focus to do well in school, and later in life, in work.

You may hyperfixate on certain things, hobbies, subjects, or even people, which might be difficult for neurotypicals to understand why you can only focus some of the time. But hyperfixations are irregular and only occur when it involves something that provides you with enough dopamine that encourages focus and attention. This means that you can't control it nor can you dictate which tasks or activities trigger it.

Another thing to consider is the inconsistency of motivation to stay focused. You might fixate on an activity, and three hours in, you lose interest. This explains why you probably have trouble finishing everything on your to-do list and why you may have multiple forgotten hobbies and uncompleted tasks because you've randomly lost interest in them.

Improving your attention span and focus will require you to experiment and find the strategies that work best for you. Some days your inattentiveness might be worse, and other days you might not have any trouble getting through the school day.

There are a few things you can try that might help keep you focused, but remember that your brain chemistry is not typical. Not being able to focus for long periods has nothing to do with your intelligence.

- Practice thought dumping.
- Distracting thoughts can be crippling when you're in a situation where you really need to stay focused. When your brain is repeatedly reminding you of that one thing you forgot to do, it can be tempting to lean into it so you don't forget again.
- A great way to get these thoughts to pipe down is getting them out of your mind by writing them down. Keep all your brain dumps in one area (a piece of paper or your phone's notes app). It can help you remain focused when you don't have to worry about trying to keep everything stored in your mind all the time. It's okay if you don't write down everything of importance in one go. You can circle back and add things when necessary.
- Interrupt yourself.

- This might sound counterintuitive, but breaking your own focus might make it easier to complete the task. Even if you set a five-minute alarm every half an hour to give you time to go to the bathroom and take a sip of water, it might create some tension or even frustration, which may enhance your focus and dedication to finishing whatever you're working on.
- You might feel anxious to get back to the task at hand as soon as possible because you want to complete it. Again, this might not work for everyone, and if you reach for your phone or any other distraction during this time, you could risk losing your focus entirely in the process.
- Remind yourself of the end goal.
- Sometimes the big picture can get lost or even forgotten in the mind of someone with ADHD or EFD. When you want to save up for a new hobby or a video gaming setup, you can have a sticky note stuck to your mirror to prevent you from forgetting what you're ultimately saving up for and spending the money impulsively.
- Take a breath.
- Once you become aware of your drifting thoughts or inattentiveness, try not to get frustrated with yourself. Instead, take a few minutes to do some deep breathing exercises, and maybe stretch out your arms and crack your knuckles (no, it does not

cause arthritis) to bring you back to the present and stimulate your mind.

- Manage your expectations.
- Training your brain to be more focused won't happen overnight. It will be slow progress and there will be setbacks, but it will ultimately be worth it. Try to remember that you can't help it, and you're doing everything you can to improve yourself. Be proud of the accomplishments you achieve and the progress you make, no matter how small they might be.

You're literally rewiring your brain here! So take it easy on yourself, and eventually, you will reap the benefits of staying consistent with your efforts.

Prioritizing and Planning

If you have ADHD or EFD, you might have trouble with planning and prioritizing since it's part of the many executive skills we have as human beings. People with ADHD and EFD struggle to categorize tasks and responsibilities and plan accordingly. They frequently feel as though there's just not enough time during the day to get everything done, so they give up.

The core principles of planning and prioritizing are urgency and importance. Urgent tasks usually mean there's a looming deadline whereas important tasks are attributed to the significance or benefits they will have in our lives. Important tasks guide us and often mirror our purposes and desired end results in life.

Understanding the relevance and importance of the task comes down to when it needs to be done, why it needs to be done, and how it makes us feel. Certain tasks or responsibilities need to be done regardless of how they make us feel, while others are less urgent or important, but they make us feel good.

One solution to this problem is creating an Eisenhower Matrix. It involves sorting all your responsibilities and tasks into four categories: urgent and important, important but not urgent, urgent but not important, and neither important nor urgent.

Drawing a table (like the one below) can help make it feel more comprehensive and easier to understand.

Quadrant 1: Do it now!

Urgent and important

You should drop everything and focus on these tasks. They can include things like:

- a crisis or emergency
- deadline
- things that happen last minute

Quadrant 2: Goals, no deadline

Important but not urgent

These are usually things that relate to your future goals and overall health such as:

- healthy habits and choices
- maintaining relationships
- personal goals
- hobbies

Quadrant 3: Interruptions

Urgent but not important

Generally speaking, these will be interruptions or responsibilities that need to be addressed but have no time limit:

- responsibilities and chores
- internal pressure to complete to-do list

Quadrant 4: Distractions

Not urgent or important

You should avoid wasting too much time doing these activities since it consists of distractions that won't benefit you in the long term:

- social media and internet browsing
- T.V or video games
- anything that distracts you from your goals

A BREAKDOWN of this table is as follows:

- If you spend too much time in Quadrant 1, you're living in crisis mode, which could be stressful and cause your ADHD symptoms to worsen.
- Quadrant 2 is the sweet spot; everything is flowing well, and you're setting realistic goals and following through with them. You're managing to keep up-to-date on all your chores and responsibilities while also taking time for yourself. A balanced lifestyle will reduce stress and keep you motivated and feeling fulfilled.
- If you're disrupting your schedule to always help others and put the needs of others above your own, you may have trouble with setting boundaries and therefore live in Quadrant 3.

- If you get easily distracted and give in to distractions to avoid doing what you're supposed to do, you get stuck in Quadrant 4, where nothing gets done. This could lead to lowered self-esteem and poor confidence since you most likely feel guilty for not completing anything on your to-do list.

You want to spend most of your time attending to tasks and responsibilities in Quadrant 2 since the others either create constant and unnecessary stress or are a waste of your time. This means not leaving projects with deadlines until it becomes extremely urgent and not spending too much time scrolling social media or playing video games.

Take some time to reflect on where you tend to land on the table. Where are you spending most of your time? And what changes can you make to spend more time living in Quadrant 2?

How to Approach Planning and Prioritizing

Start by assigning a time and importance value to all your chores and responsibilities (this includes hobbies and self-care). This is the step most people with ADHD struggle with since everything feels equally important unless there's a strict deadline or emergency involved.

It's all about what makes the most sense to you and why. Take into consideration how it will affect you in the future, why it's important, which task you usually try to avoid, and what will happen if you don't complete this task. For example:

- **Task**
- **Due Date**
- **Importance**
- **Priority number**

School project

- A week
- Good grades
- 1

Working out

- None
- Physical and mental health
- 2

Folding laundry

- None
- Room looks messy
- No space left on bed
- 3

You could also consider getting an accountability partner. Not only will you have some help with determining the importance of certain tasks, but it's also much easier to follow through with things on your to-do list when there's someone who can hold you accountable.

Some other benefits that an accountability partner can offer are studying, doing homework, working together on an assignment, and having them sit with you while you clean your room (or even help, if they're willing).

But the most important thing to remember when approaching planning and prioritizing is trial and error, patience, and persistence. Planning and prioritizing all your tasks will take up some of your time, but it's time well spent. But also, persistence will breed success and patience is crucial. Putting yourself down for failing or having setbacks will only serve you negatively.

8

GOAL SETTING AND ACHIEVEMENT

People with ADHD tend to ignore activities or tasks that don't provide an immediate reward. Long-term goals get neglected or even forgotten about even if they're something that the person really wants for their future selves.

A long-term goal usually requires you to work on it little by little every day for months or even years before achieving it. This can be demotivating to people with ADHD or EFD, so they end up not following through with the smaller, daily tasks that will eventually lead them down the road to success.

There are plenty of very famous and successful people who have ADHD, such as Bill Gates, Michael Phelps, John F. Kennedy, Jim Carrey, Simone Biles, and Emma Watson, to name a few. So there's no doubt that people with ADHD can absolutely achieve incredible things despite this sometimes crippling disorder.

Super Skills

So, how do you motivate yourself to achieve your long-term goals and commit to them even when it feels like the hardest thing to do every day?

Work on the following "super skills" to boost your confidence and motivation in the face of ADHD and EFD:

- Know your strengths.
- Years of bullying and poor grades have most definitely done some damage to your confidence and self-esteem. Maybe it's your creativity, empathy, sensitivity, or exuberance that makes you an amazing human being. There's more to life than being able to sit still and focus for the better part of the day.
- You can discover your strengths by asking yourself the following questions:
- How have I succeeded this month?
- What achievements am I most proud of?
- When do I feel most appreciated?
- What interests me the most?
- Set personal and meaningful goals.

- Without you being aware of them, you probably already have intrinsic goals that relate to your education, health, relationships, hobbies, or even a bucket list. A good goal will have some significance to you and a reason for why you want to achieve it.
- Use self-motivation.
- Because of the lack of dopamine production in the brain of someone with ADHD or EFD, motivation can be hard to come by. However, it is something that you can work on with the help of self-talk and compassion.
- Remind yourself about your past successes and achievements and understand that doing something that will benefit you in the future does not have to feel good in the moment.
- Remember that you are completely in control as you do what needs to be done. Believe that you are capable of doing things that are hard and tell yourself this as often as you need to.
- Work on emotional control.
- Emotional dysregulation is common in people with ADHD and EFD and can make life very difficult. Start by researching an emotion chart so you are better able to identify your feelings.
- Take some time every day to really evaluate what you are feeling without trying to suppress or avoid these emotions.

SMART Goals

Chances are, you've already heard of this popular acronym to help set goals that line up with your values and capabilities. SMART is an acronym that stands for: specific, measurable, achievable, realistic, and timely.

All of these characteristics are important when deciding on what you want to achieve in both the short and long term.

Breaking down goals into multiple milestones that are relatively easy to accomplish is the way to go since many small successes will not only lead to fulfilling your overall goal, but this will also improve your confidence when it comes to completing these tasks. Create a plan of action and evaluate your progress frequently to ensure you're moving towards your ultimate goal.

Specific

A goal that is vague and non-specific will set you up for failure. An example of a non-specific goal is something like "I want to save money." This is more of a statement or a wish that doesn't really provide enough motivation or incentive to follow through with it.

The more reason and details you add to your goal, the more weight is put behind the outcome. Ask yourself questions such as why do you want to save money or how much money do you want to save?

Measurable

Both short- and long-term goals will likely involve multiple steps or milestones before they can be achieved. With every step you complete or milestone you reach, you can gauge progress and ensure you're moving in the right direction.

Using the example of saving money, you might want to put aside a certain amount every week or every month depending on how much you're able to save. The progress here will be apparent as you see your money increase every time you put some aside.

Achievable

It's important that the goal is actually possible to achieve and break down into daily, weekly, or monthly steps that you can complete that will eventually get you the result you're looking for. It goes without saying that a goal that is impossible to achieve will only serve to make you feel bad about yourself.

Some questions that might help you determine if a goal is achievable are: what is the purpose of achieving your goal and is the goal worthy of pursuing?

For example, with saving money, you most likely have a valid reason for doing so such as buying a new video game, pursuing a hobby, or getting tickets to a concert.

Realistic

With all things considered, the goal also needs to be realistic, meaning that you need to have the tools or resources to be able to reach milestones and eventually achieve your end goal.

If you want to save money but you don't have any income, that's not a very realistic goal. A better goal would be to create an income in some way by monetizing your hobby or another skill you have before having a goal of saving money.

Timely

It might be a good idea to give yourself a deadline or a time frame of when you want the goal (or milestones) to be completed. This creates a sense of urgency and importance, which may provide you with enough motivation to stick to your goals.

The timeline shouldn't be too far into the future either since people with ADHD or EFD might lose interest or simply forget about it.

Saving small amounts of money for something like a video game or concert tickets shouldn't take you more than a couple of weeks, whereas bigger amounts will naturally take longer. It's also important to make the deadline or time frame realistic. Saving for a new car in the span of a few months is not realistic, for example.

Achievement

It's possible to have multiple goals that involve personal, school, social, and future career achievements. Long-term goals can be broken up into short-term milestones that will make it easier for someone with ADHD or EFD to remember and focus on.

An example of a personal goal is mastering a new skill or hobby: for school, it could be raising your grades; for your social life, it could be being yourself and making friends that accept you for who you are; and a future career goal could be getting an internship in the field you're interested in.

Once you complete one goal, think about what's next and come up with new goals based on your desires and needs. Things won't always work out the way you want them to because that's just how life is. Plans change, interests change, values evolve, and what you want now will probably not be what you want in a year. It's okay if your goals change over time based on how you're growing as a person, in fact, it's a good thing.

So be sure to circle back to your goals and check that they're still lining up with your current mindset and values and tweak them accordingly. There's really no point in holding on to a goal that you no longer care for, so don't be afraid to make some changes or alterations or choose a new goal completely. Goals should be relevant, so you're actually interested in putting in the effort to achieve them.

And lastly, be proud of every step you manage to take that leads you closer to your destination. There are many paths to take up a mountain that will lead you to the top. Some are easier than others, but the only person wasting their time is the one running around telling everyone else that their path is wrong.

READY TO LEND A HELPING HAND?

YOU KNOW BETTER than most people what it's like to live with ADHD... and it's within your power to make someone's journey a little easier.

HEAD over to Amazon and let other readers know how this book has helped you. Just one or two sentences could be enough to point someone who's struggling in the direction of the guidance they need.

WANT TO HELP OTHERS?

THANK you for helping me on my quest to make neurodivergent people feel less alone and find the guidance they need. I hope everything you've learned on your journey to this page will add to your toolbox that serves you for a lifetime.

>>> Scan above to leave your review on Amazon.

AFTERWORD

You have ADHD or EFD, that's a fact. So stop comparing yourself to people who don't have it. People who don't have a neurological disorder are living life on easy mode, and yes, that's very unfair. But life isn't fair, and there's nothing you can do about it besides accepting it.

However, coming to terms with having ADHD or EFD does not mean you have an excuse to not try to improve your life or try to manage your symptoms better. It also doesn't mean you should beat yourself up for struggling with some things. Own your traits and quirks and stop apologizing for who you are!

Some strategies will work for you, and some won't. The only way to find out is to give them a fair chance. Whether you try meditating, spending more time in nature, or adopting healthy habits, don't give up after three days because it's not giving you the results you expected.

It's not going to be easy to stick with the program, which is why you need to take it slow and steady and keep trying. Don't try and reshuffle your entire life at once, just make minor adjustments. Keep the ones that work and discard the ones that don't.

I would say the most prominent changes you need to make are the ones concerning your mental and physical well-being. So work on improving your eating habits, drinking enough water, getting enough sleep, and adding some kind of easy and enjoyable exercise activity on most days of the week.

Then, and only then, should you move on to making changes in other aspects of your life such as implementing strategies for improving your emotional regulation, being more productive, building your social life and relationships, and working on setting and achieving goals.

It's also worth taking some time to assess what's making it easy for you to procrastinate or neglect your responsibilities. And I'm willing to bet that social media is at the top of that list. There are no benefits to social media unless you're only using it to stay in contact with relatives or friends who are living far away. I'm not saying you shouldn't use social media for recreational purposes at all, but when you're dealing with something like ADHD or EFD, limiting the time you spend on it is near impossible.

While adopting and sticking with healthier habits are more difficult for people who are neurodiverse, they're not impossible when you utilize practical strategies, set reminders, have someone to hold you accountable, and replace unhelpful habits with better ones.

Hobbies and small tasks can really help with social media addiction. Instead of reaching for your phone when you're bored or trying to avoid starting on a chore, try working on a hobby or starting on a smaller, easier task and use that momentum to keep you going.

Avoid distractions like your phone or the T.V. while you're taking a break, instead build the anticipation by doing nothing for a few minutes before getting back to what you were doing. Keeping your environment tidy and organized also helps avoid distractions and encourages focus.

The hardest part of completing tasks is getting started. There are many ways to hack this obstacle such as the five-minute rule or starting on an easy task and using that momentum to move on to the next task. Wear shoes (preferably sneakers or boots) in the house, and don't take them off since your brain tends to associate taking off your shoes with you being done for the day. When a hyperfixation period hits, use that energy to get as much done as possible.

Use your current values and interests to create goals that are realistic. Break your goals down into smaller, less intimidating milestones that will provide you with a sense of accomplishment to keep your determination going. And don't forget to evaluate your progress often so you don't stray from the desired end result.

Remember to not be too hard on yourself—as long as you remain determined to improve yourself, you will get there eventually. Progress isn't always linear, and sometimes we lose sight of our goals or our destination changes completely along the way. As long as you focus on improvement, you will never fail.

Stay consistent with your efforts as much as you can, and use the tools and strategies explained in this book to guide you along the way. If you found this book helpful, kindly leave a review on Amazon.

BIBLIOGRAPHY

Abdalla, S. (n.d.). *How I beat my social media habit (and how you can too)*. Understood. https://www.understood.org/en/articles/how-i-beat-my-social-media-habit-and-how-you-can-too

ADD Resource Center. (2017, September 4). *Setting target goals for managing ADHD symptoms*. https://www.addrc.org/setting-target-goals-for-adhd/

ADHD Army. (2021, May 5). *Social media can be toxic for people with ADHD—so I decided to disconnect*. ADHD Army. https://adhdarmy.com/social-media-is-toxic-for-people-with-adhd-so-disconnect-from-it/

ADHD Clinic. (n.d.). *ADHD in social situations; attention deficit hyperactivity disorder*. The ADHD Clinic. https://adhdclinic.co.uk/adhd-in-social-situations/

Akin, T. S. (2019, October 22). *Executive functioning : What is inhibition?* Chicago Home Tutor. https://chicagohometutor.com/blog/executiving-functioning-inhibition

Al-Saad, M. S. H., Al-Jabri, B., & Almarzouki, A. F. (2021, July 21). A review of working memory training in the management of attention deficit hyperactivity disorder. *Frontiers in Behavioral Neuroscience, 15*. https://doi.org/10.3389/fnbeh.2021.686873

Bethel, S. (n.d.). *Inhibition: executive functions*. https://www.stephaniebethany.com/blog/inhibition-executive-functions

Blanchfield, T. (2022, February 28). *How does caffeine affect people with ADHD?* Verywell Mind. https://www.verywellmind.com/how-does-caffeine-affect-people-with-adhd-5217867

Broadbent, E. (2019, October 16). My ADD sabotages my social skills online. *ADDitude*. https://www.additudemag.com/adhd-problems-with-social-media/

Center on the Developing Child. (n.d.). *Executive function activities for adolescents.*   https://46y5eh11fhgw3ve3ytpwxt9r-wpengine.netdna-ssl.com/wp-content/uploads/2015/05/Activities-for-Adolescents.pdf

Centers for Disease Control and Prevention. (2019). *ADHD in the classroom.* https://www.cdc.gov/ncbddd/adhd/school-success.html

Centers for Disease Control and Prevention. (2021, September 23). *What is ADHD?* https://www.cdc.gov/ncbddd/adhd/facts.html

CHADD. (2018). *Treatment of teens with ADHD.* https://chadd.org/for-parents/treatment-of-teens-with-adhd/

Chatterjee, R. (2018, July 17). *More screen time for teens linked to ADHD symptoms.* NPR.org. https://www.npr.org/sections/health-shots/2018/07/17/629517464/more-screen-time-for-teens-may-fuel-adhd-symptoms

Cherry, K. (2019). *How to improve your self-control.* Verywell Mind. https://www.verywellmind.com/psychology-of-self-control-4177125

The Chesapeake Center. (n.d.). *Healthy daily habits to reduce ADHD symptoms.* https://chesapeakeadd.com/home/education-and-training/articles/healthy-daily-habits-to-reduce-adhd-symptoms/

Childs, C. (2007, April 2). *Eat the frogs first—A guide to prioritizing.* Lifehack. https://www.lifehack.org/articles/productivity/eat-the-frogs-first-a-guide-to-prioritizing.html

Chronister, K. (2021, June 19). *Best activities for teens with ADHD.* Key Transitions. https://keytransitions.com/activities-for-teens-with-adhd/

D'Souza, A. A., Moradzadeh, L., & Wiseheart, M. (2018). Musical training, bilingualism, and executive function: Working memory and inhibitory control. *Cognitive Research: Principles and Implications,* 3(1), 11. https://doi.org/10.1186/s41235-018-0095-6

Davenport, B. (2019, September 11). *Being the boss of your brain.* Institute for Couple and Family Enhancement. https://www.icfetx.com/blog/136902-being-the-boss-of-your-brain

Earnest, A. (2020, August 24). *ADHD 12 step: How to form habits that stick.* Invisible Illness. https://medium.com/invisible-illness/adhd-12-step-how-to-form-habits-that-stick-15ceab22c752

Finch, S. D. (2020, August 31). *ADHD quick tips: 11 focus boosts when your brain won't cooperate.* Healthline. https://www.healthline.com/health/mental-health/adhd-quick-focus-boosts

Franklin, S. (2017, November 7). *5 types of self-care for your mental health.* The Mighty. https://themighty.com/topic/mental-health/types-of-self-care-for-mental-health

Gillette, H. (2021, June 24). *Tips on how to focus with ADHD.* Psych Central. https://psychcentral.com/adhd/adhd-tips-to-fire-up-your-focus

Goldman, R. (2015). *14 adult ADHD signs and symptoms.* Healthline. https://www.healthline.com/health/adhd/adult-adhd

Greenblatt, J. M. (2022, April 13). *Why mindfulness works so well for ADHD.* Finally Focused. https://finallyfocused.org/why-mindfulness-meditation-works-adhd-studies/

Gysi, S. (2016, August 3). *Video games can be good for brain health?* BOLD. https://bold.expert/video-games-can-be-good-for-brain-health/

Hersh, E. (2020, August 17). *Sleep hygiene explained and 10 tips for better sleep.* Healthline. https://www.healthline.com/health/sleep-hygiene#what-is-it

Hjalmarsdottir, F. (2020, January 30). Does nutrition play a role in ADHD? Healthline. https://www.healthline.com/nutrition/nutrition-and-adhd

Holland, K. (2018, May 18). *Personal hygiene: Benefits, creating a routine, in kids, and more.* Healthline. https://www.healthline.com/health/personal-hygiene#

Honos-Webb, L. (2021, July 9). 6 secrets to goal setting with ADHD. *ADDitude.* https://www.additudemag.com/achieving-personal-goals-adhd/amp/

Hoshaw, C. (2021, April 16). *30 mindfulness activities to help you find calm at any age.* Healthline. https://www.healthline.com/health/mind-body/mindfulness-activities

Jaska, P. (n.d.). *The disorganized adult.* ADHD Center. https://www.add-centers.com/articles/the-disorganized-adult

Jones, H. (2022, January 12). *Can ADHD cause problems with memory?*

Verywell Health. https://www.verywellhealth.com/can-adhd-cause-memory-issues-5207991

Kim. (2021, May 28). *13 ways to stop being a people-pleaser.* Clay Behavioral Health Center. https://ccbhc.org/13-ways-to-stop-being-a-people-pleaser/

Kokkoris, M. D., & Stavrova, O. (2020, January 16). The dark side of self-control. *Harvard Business Review.* https://hbr.org/2020/01/the-dark-side-of-self-control

Laderer, A. (2020, October 2). *The best diet for people with ADHD: Foods to eat and avoid.* Insider. https://www.insider.com/guides/health/mental-health/adhd-diet

Levine, H. (2022, January 17). *Meditation and yoga for ADHD.* WebMD. https://www.webmd.com/add-adhd/adhd-mindfulness-meditation-yoga

Low, K. (2021, February 24). *Problem solving for adults with ADHD.* Verywell Mind. https://www.verywellmind.com/steps-to-problem-solving-for-adults-with-adhd-20407

Cummins, M.. (2013, March 7). *Improving task initiation when you have ADHD.* Marla Cummins. https://marlacummins.com/adhd-initiation-getting-started/

Miller, K. (2020, January 30). *What is self-control theory in psychology?* PositivePsychology.com. https://positivepsychology.com/self-control-theory/

NHS. (2018, May 30). *Symptoms—attention deficit hyperactivity disorder (ADHD).* https://www.nhs.uk/conditions/attention-deficit-hyperactivity-disorder-adhd/symptoms/

Oscar-Berman, M., Blum, K., Chen, T. J., Braverman, E., Waite, R., Downs, W., Arcuri, V., Notaro, A., Palomo, T., & Comings, D. (2008). Attention-deficit-hyperactivity disorder and reward deficiency syndrome. *Neuropsychiatric Disease and Treatment, 4(5),* 893. https://doi.org/10.2147/ndt.s2627

The OT Toolbox. (2017, March 3). *Task initiation executive functioning strategies.* The OT Toolbox. https://www.theottoolbox.com/task-initiation-executive-functioning-strategies/

Peterson, T. J. (n.d.). *10 best ADHD self-help strategies*. HealthyPlace. https://www.healthyplace.com/self-help/adhd/10-best-adhd-self-help-strategies

Porter, E. (2012, December 17). *Learn the triggers for your ADHD symptoms*. Healthline. https://www.healthline.com/health/adhd/adhd-trigger-symptoms

Psychology Today Staff. (n.d.-a). Executive function. *Psychology Today*. https://www.psychologytoday.com/us/basics/executive-function#improving-executive-function

Psychology Today Staff. (n.d.-b). Growth mindset. *Psychology Today*. https://www.psychologytoday.com/us/basics/growth-mindset

Ra, C. K., Cho, J., Stone, M. D., De La Cerda, J., Goldenson, N. I., Moroney, E., Tung, I., Lee, S. S., & Leventhal, A. M. (2018). Association of digital media use with subsequent symptoms of attention-deficit/hyperactivity disorder among adolescents. *JAMA Network*, 320(3), 255. https://doi.org/10.1001/jama.2018.8931

Rawe, J. (n.d.). *The ADHD brain*. Understood. https://www.understood.org/en/articles/adhd-and-the-brain

Raypole, C. (2020, April 28). *How to control your emotions: 11 strategies to try*. Healthline. https://www.healthline.com/health/how-to-control-your-emotions

Raypole, C. (2021, January 8). *How to control your mind: 10 techniques*. Healthline. https://www.healthline.com/health/mental-health/how-to-control-your-mind

Rodden, J. (2017, February 17). What is executive dysfunction? Signs and symptoms of EFD. *ADDitude*. https://www.additudemag.com/what-is-executive-function-disorder/

Sabater, V. (2020, December 10). *Definition and characteristics of cognitive rigidity*. Exploring Your Mind. https://exploringyourmind.com/definition-and-characteristics-of-cognitive-rigidity/

Saline, S. (2021, September 15). *Planning and prioritizing practices for ADHD brains: What's the plan, and when do you start?!* Dr. Sharon Saline. https://drsharonsaline.com/2021/09/14/planning-and-prioritizing-practices-for-adhd-brains-whats-the-plan-and-when-do-you-start/

Sharma, S., Arain, M., Mathur, P., Rais, A., Nel, W., Sandhu, R., Haque, M., & Johal, L. (2013). Maturation of the adolescent brain. *Neuropsychiatric Disease and Treatment, 9*(9), 449–461. https://doi.org/10.2147/ndt.s39776

Silny, J. (2015, July 21). *7 ways to take control of your mind*. ADD Resource Center. https://www.addrc.org/7-ways-to-take-control-of-your-mind/

Smith, M. (2019). *ADHD and school*. Help Guide. https://www.helpguide.org/articles/add-adhd/attention-deficit-disorder-adhd-and-school.htm

Stafford, S. (2011, May 10). *Self-control may be a key factor to success*. PsychAlive. https://www.psychalive.org/self-control-may-be-a-key-factor-to-success/

Stenger, M. (2017, April 11). *7 ways to develop cognitive flexibility*. InformED. https://www.opencolleges.edu.au/informed/features/7-ways-develop-cognitive-flexibility/

Stewart, K. (2013, December 16). *How exercise works like a drug for ADHD*. Everyday Health. https://www.everydayhealth.com/add-adhd/can-you-exercise-away-adhd-symptoms.aspx

Tartakovsky, M. (2014, March 15). *10 daily habits that help you manage ADHD*. Psych Central. https://psychcentral.com/blog/10-daily-habits-that-help-you-manage-adhd#1

Thomas, L. (2019, February 26). *How does ADHD affect the brain?* News-Medical.net. https://www.news-medical.net/health/How-does-ADHD-Affect-the-Brain.aspx

Tiimo. (n.d.). *ADHD and task initiation: Getting the ball rolling*. https://www.tiimoapp.com/blog/adhd-task-initiation/

Tuckman, A. (2019, July 30). ADHD minds are trapped in now (& other time management truths). *ADDitude*. https://www.additudemag.com/time-management-skills-adhd-brain/

Verlaet, A., Maasakkers, C., Hermans, N., & Savelkoul, H. (2018). Rationale for dietary antioxidant treatment of ADHD. *Nutrients, 10*(4), 405. https://doi.org/10.3390/nu10040405

Whyte, A. (2019, January 2). *Ten hobbies for teens that aren't sports,*

computers, or gaming. Evolve Treatment Centers. https://evolvetreat
ment.com/blog/hobbies-teens/

Your day is getting better — Starting now. (2022, April 15). ADDitude.
https://www.additudemag.com/slideshows/adhd-famous-quotes-for-a-
bad-day/

Printed in Great Britain
by Amazon

46737272R00099